THE FAKE FACTOR

The Fake Factor

Why we love brands but buy fakes

Sarah McCartney

First published in 2005 by:

Marshall Cavendish Business
An imprint of Marshall Cavendish International (Asia) Private Limited
A member of Times Publishing Limited
Times Centre, 1 New Industrial Road
Singapore 536196
T: +65 6213 9300
F: +65 6285 4871
E: te@sg.marshallcavendish.com
Online bookstore: www.marshallcavendish.com/genref

and

Cyan Communications Limited
119 Wardour Street
London W1F 0UW
United Kingdom
T: +44 (0)20 7565 6120
E: sales@cyanbooks.com
www.cyanbooks.com

A CIP record for this book is available from the British Library

ISBN 981 261 817 1 (Asia & ANZ)
ISBN 1-904879-42-X (Rest of world)

Designed and typeset by Curran Publishing Services, Norwich, UK
Printed and bound in Singapore

For Alan and Beryl McCartney and Elizabeth Bain

CONTENTS

Acknowledgments   *ix*

1   Tribute brands   1

2   Copycat ethics   9

3   What exactly is a brand?   17

4   Separation may occur   25

5   Extension, stretching, and snapping   29

6   The promises brands make   37

7   Real stories about fakes   45

8   Brand loyalty: Why do we feel affection for a
    "thing"?   59

9   What you say and what I hear   63

10 Brands and their logos   73

11 Minimizing risk   77

12 People do weird things while abroad   81

13 Is this the real thing?   93

CONTENTS

14 An Internet adventure   99

15 Cabbage and the European trainer mountain   109

16 The earner–spender generation   119

17 When greed was good   125

18 Labeled with love   133

19 Work hard, play hard, sell your grandmother   141

20 Intellectual property law and international
    ethics – by a non-lawyer   145

21 Expand your market: copy your own brand   157

22 Is creativity cool?   167

23 Handbags at dawn   175

24 Mavens and magazines   181

25 Shopping: a new world hobby   189

26 Maintenance and desire   197

27 Brand damage: counterfeits or customers?   205

28 Is it serious?   213

Notes   221
Bibliography   223
Index   225

ACKNOWLEDGMENTS

Thanks to Nick Randell, Judy Lui, Beryl McCartney, John Simmons, Neil Fletcher, Marietta Pacella, Pom, Martin, and Linette at Cyan Books, and everyone who joined in with the research.

Thanks also to the staff of Boldon Comprehensive School, Boldon Colliery, Tyne and Wear, especially Mr. Halverson, Mr. Barker, Mr. Lee, Mr. Loane, Mr. Williams, Mr. Robson, and Mr. Grieveson (without whom we would never have learned the meaning of really hard work).

1
Tribute brands

Take a collection of books about brands and you will observe that they can be neatly divided into two piles. The first contains "How to" guides which advise businesses on the best ways to sell things to their customers. The second are anti-business, shock exposés of the ways in which gullible consumers are manipulated by cynical businesses into senseless consumerism. You have "Brands are great, let's sell them to people" versus "Brands are wicked, let's boycott them." This book stays seated firmly on the fence; I think you get a better view.

Brands exist; people who market them can behave well or badly. Buyers' motives vary too. Business is about making enough profit to stay in business; sometimes that includes copying other people's business ideas. Whether or not businesses break the law in order to do that depends on three elements. Is there a ready market for their products; are their potential customers happy to buy illegal fakes or unaware that they are doing so? Will the risks of getting caught outweigh the potential for making a profit? Do their culture's business ethics or their own sense of personal morality allow them to steal other people's intellectual property? Countries' widely differing laws, their interpretation, and their enforcement are influential but variable.

At the Musée de la Contrefaçon in Paris there is a 2000-year-old terracotta wine jar seal. Some Ancient Romans pressed identifying text into their seals after filling their jars with wine. Illiterate counterfeiters made marks which looked a bit like writing in order to fool their equally illiterate customers into believing they were buying the genuine article on the cheap. Making fakes and selling them as the real thing is not new, but in the twenty-first century it is booming. We find ourselves in a world where the risks have been dwarfed by the temptations of potential profits. How did that happen?

The best current estimates reckon that counterfeiting accounts for up to 7 percent of all world trade. That's more counterfeits than legitimate trade in clothes or cars. Cigarettes dominate with 44 percent of the total market for counterfeit goods, judging by the shipments which the US Customs and Border Protection department has seized and confiscated.[1] Several million counterfeit cigarettes are estimated to be sold each day in the United Kingdom. The UK's ITV News reported in December 2004:

> Frightening new figures have revealed that black market counterfeit cigarettes can contain far higher levels of toxic chemicals – like arsenic and lead – than regular ones. One million fake cigarettes are seized by the authorities across Britain every day but that's only a fraction of the counterfeit market. 85 percent of cigarettes sold on the cheap, in shops and on the street, are fake and they're ten times as damaging as "real" cigarettes.[2]

After cigarettes, the second biggest at haul in 2003 by US Customs was clothing (14 percent) and the third (12 percent) was for handbags, wallets, and backpacks (their classification). Another 9 percent was made up of watches, sunglasses, footwear, and headwear. This massive counterfeit clothing and accessory market is the one which I have given most attention; it is a booming business; organized crime gangs are believed to be giving up drugs (too risky) in favor of fashion items which can be openly sold on city streets to willing buyers without attracting much police attention.

Back to the Musée, which my friend and I were visiting for two reasons; Judy was writing her design studies dissertation on the effect of counterfeiting on luxury brands and I was helping with her research, with a view to collecting material to add to this book. The museum is a small, venerable institution run by the Union des Fabricants, the French manufacturers' association; the Vuitton family name features on the carved wooden panel showing past chairmen. In the elegant Parisian villa which houses their collection we saw some astonishingly good rip-offs including Christian Dior, Gucci, Lacoste, and Louis Vuitton clothes and accessories, plus counterfeit Lea & Perrins Worcestershire Sauce, Perrier water, Mumm Cordon Rouge, Laughing Cow cheeses and – something which scared the socks off me – fake Renault car parts, and cheap, potentially lethal copies of children's toys. Until that point my personal experience of counterfeits had been in luxury goods.

I found tales of many other counterfeit products while researching this book. They included trademarked drugs, computers, Olympic Games souvenirs, Manchester United, Marrakech, and Montevideo football shirts, Levis jeans, Cartier and Chopard watches, Oakley and Dior sunglasses, Duracell batteries, "antique" furniture from India, "champagne" from Leeds, washing powder which caused skin burns, whisky in Manchester, vodka in Doncaster, Harry Potter books in China, passports, car tax discs, disabled parking permits, Van Goghs, diamonds (apparently "Moisannite" is such a good fake that jewelers are having trouble telling the difference), Don Bradman cricket memorabilia, Timberland boots, Armani clothes, Guerlain, Elizabeth Arden, and Givenchy perfume, CDs, DVDs, DVD players, British gold sovereigns in Greece, Hermès scarves, Ralph Lauren polo shirts, mobile phone accessories, Von Dutch hats, Nike t-shirts, satellite TV smartcards, money, the Burberry check on numerous items, Canon cameras, Adidas shoes, Tetley tea bags, fake Smurfs in Belgium, and a whole industry manufacturing "antiquities" in Pakistan. Handbags are the stars of the counterfeit world: Fendi, Louis Vuitton, Kate Spade, Gucci, Dior – anything easily recognizable and priced to be unavailable to 999 out of 1000 handbag purchasers will be copied in quantity and supplied to fulfill the demand.

Two top tales which are outstanding for their "what if?" quality were the stories about fake electronics sold to the Pentagon, destined for the Hawk missile guidance system but intercepted before they could be put to harm, and the news report about a seized consignment of counterfeit, low-quality condoms.

In intellectual property law, seriously hazardous fakes are known as "safety critical goods." These include cigarettes, alcohol, medicines, children's toys, and food. In 2003 at least 13 babies, possibly as many as 50, died from being fed counterfeit formula baby milk with 1 percent of the nutritional value of the brand it copied. Investigators found 171 babies in the Chinese province of Anhui suffering from malnutrition while their mothers believed they were feeding them adequately. Lack of money, choice, and information put people in developing countries at risk from buying life-threatening goods masquerading behind stolen brand names.

Where Western prices make branded goods impossibly out of reach to all but the wealthiest citizens, copies fill the gaps, especially in the case of easily pirated electronic media. In Vietnam pirated software takes almost 100 percent of the market. Pirated CDs, DVDs, and VCDs are reckoned to account for 90 percent of the market in China, the Philippines, and Indonesia.

The ethics of trading in counterfeit handbags are on an entirely different scale from manufacturing and selling life-threatening products which is one of the reasons why the business has been allowed to spread so rapidly. However, counterfeiters' profits are believed to be funding equally life-threatening criminal activity, but at several steps removed. One of Interpol's current headaches is that the shopping public thinks counterfeit handbags are not such a terrible thing – only a tiny bit illegal and not really doing anyone any harm – which is why criminals are making easy profits from pirating and counterfeiting. There is a willing market for fake watches and polo shirts; while the products themselves aren't going to kill anyone, the profits from selling them, the authorities report, are financing terrorism and used for money laundering. This is not mere homeland security hype. In Europe the biggest business in counterfeiting is in Italy and Northern Ireland amongst active terrorist groups.

With branded clothing and accessories, where the copied manufacturers are concerned mainly with lost profits, damage to their brand's identity, and infringement of their intellectual property rights, the legal authorities are much more alarmed by the activities which the counterfeiters' profits are funding.

Although China and Russia currently lead the field in the world counterfeiting league, fake goods are made everywhere that manufacturing capability exists and people aren't troubled by ethics in their quest for profits. It's not one-way traffic; a British company killed air travelers by supplying fake aircraft parts to Singapore and the Kenyan coffee crop was devastated by a substandard counterfeit fungicide from Europe. In 2003 ITN reported:

> A recent survey from the United States named 44 countries as producers of fake goods including every member of the EU and the US itself.
>
> The EU calculates that 39 percent of the trade in software and data processing products within the European single market is counterfeit, 16 percent of audio-visual goods are fake and between 10 to 16 percent of clothing and textile products are counterfeit.[3]

In developing countries where distribution of European and American branded goods is spread thinly or unheard of, buyers may buy low-quality copies without suspecting that they are putting themselves in danger. These people may not have an option – they either buy the fake part for the village bus, or the bus doesn't work at all. What they buy is not a matter of personal choice.

In the West, when we want to buy something, we are fortunate to have a choice between a range of brands at different prices and the counterfeit option too. Why go for the counterfeits? This is the topic that I have set out to explore.

In the United Kingdom it is legal for a pedestrian to cross urban roads wherever and whenever it is safe without waiting for the green man's invitation. In relaxed, tolerant, friendly Denmark I started to cross a Copenhagen street. The little man was red, but there was no traffic in sight in either direction. Before I had taken two paces from the kerb, I heard gasps of astonishment from the little group waiting with me. So horrified were they, that I turned round, came back, and waited with them, clearly holding my British newspaper in full view so that they could see I was foreign and knew no better. In London you can pick out foreigners; they are the ones who wait for no apparent reason.

Mind you, if the driver of a car were to jump a red light, even though there were no vehicles heading in its direction, a traffic camera in the United Kingdom would take a photograph and impose a fine. I've been driven in countries where no one takes a blind bit of notice. A friend of mine driving in the Middle East was crashed into by a car heading straight out of a side road into his coach. My chum was fined for causing the accident, because if he'd stayed in the United Kingdom the accident would never have happened, the judge decided. Depending on your cultural background you may understand the law entirely differently from the way the person standing next to you interprets it.

If your school has just saved up for its first computer and you find that the software you need costs another six months worth of fund-raising, what do you do? Do you break the law and borrow someone else's copy, or do you wait? No one sees counterfeiting from the same point of view; even intellectual property lawyers manage to put over two entirely different views of the same case where the same facts are involved.

Why does a woman spend £50 on a fake Chanel handbag which could fall to bits after a couple of months when she could pay £40 for one which will last ten years from the chap at the local craft market who made it to his own design? What would you do?

A brand's reputation, despite or because of all its associated press coverage, celebrity endorsement, advertising, word-of-mouth support, and status in the eyes of its customers, still depends on the quality of the goods which bear its name. A brand is shorthand for a guarantee, a promise to its customer. Counterfeits purloin a brand and break the promise it makes. We know that fakes lie to us; why do people buy them all the same? Is it just because we love to think that we've found a bargain? ("It looks just like the real thing but it only cost me a tenner!") Or is it because the quality has become less important to us than the image?

What has happened in recent times to change us from a society which saved for the future and counted the pennies until we could afford what we wanted, into a credit card-toting, financially suicidal bunch of me-toos destined for poverty in our inadequately pensioned old age, so desperate for the latest "look" that we'll ignore the law to have it?

In December 2004 Westminster Council set up a market stall in London's Oxford Street to warn shoppers of the wide range of counterfeit goods available. Crowds gathered round and the table was inundated with people offering to buy pirated DVDs, substandard perfumes, cheap copies of football shirts, counterfeit cameras, replica Ralph Lauren sweatshirts, and fake Burberry luggage and scarves. "But they are fake!" said the Westminster Council trading standards officers. "Yeah, how much do you want for them?" replied London's bargain hunters.

Why?

2
Copycat ethics

In Havana you can scarcely set foot outside your hotel foyer on the scorching hot street before someone offers you cigars for sale. I bumped into one particular vendor so many times, and told her on each occasion that I really didn't want any cigars, that we ended up having a coffee and a chat about life in general and spending some time together. She negotiated with taxis, in restaurants, and for fresh lobster straight from the sea and got Cuban prices; I paid for both of us, thus spending around 25 percent of what I would have paid if I'd been spotted as a lone tourist. I saw a lot more of real Cuban life than I would have with the Intourist trained (and rapidly retrained) state guides, in a country where it is still technically illegal to speak to a foreigner without the proper authority. Sharing her expertise as an illegal cigar dealer, she told me that the really cheap ones which tourists could buy on the streets at $5 for 25, were made from dried banana leaves, not tobacco. The dealers will tell you that their uncles work at the cigar factories and that these are their own personal allowance. Non-smokers take them home for their cigar-aficionado friends who are devastated to find that their mates traveled that far and brought home a worthless pile of dried banana.

If you want real ones they can be bought, but not for $5 a box. My friend told me that when tourists insist on the "real thing" for less than $25 – because they have heard that this is the going rate and "absolutely refuse to be ripped off" – then what they get is a the full counterfeit presentation: convincingly ripped-off box, with the genuine fake seals, full of dried banana leaf cigars. If they had only agreed to fork out a little more they could have had the genuine article. Whose fault is it that they got fakes? After all, they could have walked over the road to the Partagas factory shop and bought them for around 10 percent of the European retail price. If buyers are greedy enough to want something for almost nothing, then can you blame the vendor for giving them what they pay for? Both parties are behaving immorally: the vendor is lying and the buyer is cheating.

Incidentally, if you were to take your permitted allowance of Cohiba Cuban cigars into Canada or the United Kingdom this is perfectly legal. Take them into the United States and you're breaking the law; fines go up to $55,000. On the other hand if you were to buy Cohibas made in the Dominican Republic they are legal in the United States. The Cubans and the Dominicans both claim the trademark and do not recognize the others' rights to use it. The Cubans claim that the Dominican Republic cigars are made with the wrong tobacco grown on the wrong soil under the wrong climatic conditions, and that calling them Cohibas is a travesty. The users of the Dominican Republic brand claim that all the cigar rolling experts left Cuba when the Batista government was booted out by Castro's gang, so the Cuban Cohibas are not manufactured with sufficient expertise. Which ones are real Cohibas and which ones are fakes? Given the choice, I'd smoke the Cubans. One of the problems with deciding what's right and what's wrong in the world of copying and counterfeiting is that the law can go either way, depending on whose territory you're standing.

Counterfeiting and copying are both difficult to prove in intellectual property law even if they seem blatantly obvious to anyone with eyes and a brain. Counterfeiting is the unauthorized manufacture of goods which carry another company's trademark or use its copyrighted designs to convince a buyer that they are the genuine branded article. Copying involves the use of other people's designs and it can be called imitation, inspiration, or interpretation to make it sound less like nicking someone else's ideas.

In the United States the fashion industry is exempt from copyright law, but not from infringing trademarks. Infringing a dress design wouldn't be illegal as long as you don't copy the logo. Try it with a branded toothpaste pack and the intellectual property lawyers would be storming your building.

One of my chums had a job which took her to Paris and Milan to buy up ready-to-wear collections; she would carefully take the clothes to pieces, copy the cut and have them manufactured in cheaper fabric for a major UK retailer. Another friend's role was to look around the fashion business for trends and recreate them for a mid-market clothing brand. It happens all the time. Copying has happened in fashion for as long as there has been fashion. One slightly romantic view, popularized by the chain stores' PR departments, is that the only way most people can follow fashion is for high street retailers to set out, Robin Hood-like, and seize new styles so that they can share them with the poor and needy; redistribution of the wealth of ideas which are generated by fat multinationals at the couture end of the business. The whole disposable fashion trend is built on this belief; disposable fashion, designed to last a few outings and washes, following the bang, slap, up-to-the-minute latest styles are whipped sharply into the high streets and last a week or two, to be replaced by next new thing.

A manufacturer with a successful product can be pretty certain that another manufacturer will make something suspiciously similar which is sold more cheaply. That's one thing which in this uncertain business world of short product lives and rapid technological advances that we can rely on with confidence. One of the reasons a copy can sell for less is that the person doing the copying has not invested any time or money in the idea. It can take years to get a product right and companies at the cutting edge of design will be paying their designers designer-style wages to have them come up with a bounty of brand new ideas.

Innovation takes investment in time, money, and usually quite a bit of both.

To put it simply, the people who put the money up want to earn back the cost of their investment or else they won't be able to afford to develop anything new; their company will fail to compete with its rivals and may tumble swiftly out of business. When you're buying from an innovative organization, some of the price you pay will include development costs. This all seems perfectly fair; the people who took the risks and put in the time, ideas, and money should expect a reward. No doubt my experience working with an innovative company which unearths new copycats on a weekly basis has colored my views, but this is also enshrined in the law based on the principles of John Locke: all people should have a right to the fruits of their labor. Mind you, try telling that to a customer who wants to buy a stylish new bag: "You can have the £100 item from the people who designed it, or you can have the £50 version from the people who copied it." This is the perennial problem for the innovators. Customers don't usually purchase with the rights and just desserts of the designers and developers in mind.

Someone who copies a business idea only invests enough time and money to steal it, nowhere near as much as it cost to develop.

Here is Philip Green, owner of the Arcadia Group including Burton, Dorothy Perkins, Miss Selfridge, Topshop, Topman, and Etam plus Bhs in the United Kingdom, quoted in the UK newspaper *The Guardian,* on the way he made his first million by rescuing a bankrupt business he had just bought:

> Then I had a look at the business. I could see what had happened. The usual. Same issues you see today. Bad buying, no discipline, no control, old stock, indecision, time-wasting, corporate thinking. I flew to Paris, shopped the shops, three suitcases of merchandise, went to Hong Kong, got it all copied, flew in, restocked the shops, got all the creditors reflowed, and got the business back to breaking even in four months.[4]

As far as the redoubtable Mr. Green is concerned there would be no question of buying in a team of designers to create a new range. Why bother? The range he wanted already existed in a more expensive form in Paris. It is standard retail practice to make exclusive designs available to those who don't have exclusive budgets. Often this is the accepted view, even if those who are being copied don't exactly find it acceptable. It is the way that the fashion industry works. However, it's tough for young independents, newly out of college and still full of ideals, to find that the high street stores have ripped off their designs too!

Here's a view collected from our web survey:

> I think a lot of the items we see in shops are "fakes" and we don't realise. I think a lot of the work of young designers is copied and sold in shops. For example I saw a gorgeous scarf in [high street retailer]. Woven cotton. I know of a CSM [Central St. Martin's] graduate who made the "originals." Hers are a different colour combination and are produced by her, they cost about three times the amount as the [high street] ones. I am sure this happens all the time. If I was a young designer I would be worried about having an "open studio."

There are ways to survive as an innovator in fashion, like bringing out a collaborative collection with a high street retailer, of which more later. Another way is to keep on innovating, looking forwards, not allowing the people who "borrow" your ideas to take up too much of your emotional energy. Here is a view from another research respondent with more fashion knowledge than the majority:

> Well, fashion comes with a natural trickle down factor. The majority of what you see on the runway

14

eventually hits the high street shops in one varia-
tion or another. That's inevitable, and I don't necessarily think it's a bad thing. So, along those lines,
I'd buy similar styles in a lesser brand as long as it's
not trying to specifically replicate the original to
the point of looking like a collection wannabe.

Having similar traits or characteristics isn't the
same as being an imitation. There's a clear difference between inspiration and imitation. I have no
problem with a trickle down of inspiration. That
trickle down is an integral aspect of the fashion
industry; without it, 90 percent of the population
would be forced to walk around naked (and that's
a bit more than 100 percent of us could stomach,
I'm afraid.)

I can't think of anything specific because I've
never bought anything that was an absolute imitation. Similar in style, yes. For example, I bought a
tweed J. Jill jacket with unfinished edges similar in
concept to what they marked at Chanel in the A03
collection. However, the jacket itself is distinctly J.
Jill and not Chanel. So again, it's the difference
between inspiration and imitation.

But how does our writer know what is typically Chanel or
distinctly J. Jill? That's down to the success of their brand
identities.

3
What exactly is a brand?

Brands are tricky things to pin down; everyone thinks they know what one is but not everyone can come up with a good definition. In my experience many people who make their living working with brands are still not entirely certain what one is.

When people talk about brands they often mean the identities of products and services that are available to buy, but political parties, charities, and people have their own brand identities too. A brand's owners will use branding techniques to persuade observers to see their brands exactly the way they would like us to see them. No one will ever see a brand in quite the same way as someone else, as our views always depends on our own experience, tastes, and culture. All an organization needs is for enough of us to agree with it, to buy into its message, and hand over our cash for it to stay in business.

One of the research questions I wrote to provide information for this book (and for Judy's dissertation) asked, "What are your favorite clothing and accessory brands? Please list up to ten."

One person replied:

> shoes, bags, earrings, necklaces, belts, trousers, skirts.

These are not brands; these are articles of clothing and accessories. The same list as brands could read:

> Adidas, Head, Claire's Accessories, Monsoon, Next, Wrangler, Top Shop.

For someone with a considerable disposable income or credit limit it could read:

> Jimmy Choo, Louis Vuitton, Tiffany, Garrard, Versace, Evisu, Dolce & Gabbana.

All these brands are the names of designers, manufacturers, or retailers; you will find their names on labels inside and possibly outside their products and they may also have a recognizable – and probably trademarked – symbol or logo sewn, printed, or attached to them.

If you are a manufacturer, large or small, and you make something of which you are justifiably proud, then it is only reasonable to put your name or your mark on it so that people will remember what to ask for when they want another one or if their friends decide they would like one too. Perhaps you paint in a certain style, then sign your art work. (Picasso's signature was so recognizable that Citroen cars recently used it on one of their models.) The style, the name, and the signature are part of the brand.

Brands were invented to identify livestock. Heat a branding iron in a fire then stamp your own mark on the hindquarters of your new cows then if someone rustles them, you can saddle up, get on your horse, ride off with your boys, and claim it back again. These days we have intellectual property law.

I like to use my former marketing professor's definition of a brand: Here are the first words of Chapter One of *Branding in Action* by Graham Hankinson and Philippa Cowking:

> A brand is a product or service made distinct by its positioning relative to the competition and by its personality.[5]

It doesn't work for all brands – sometimes you have to adapt it, with charities for instance – but it is helpful so it's a fine place to start.

A product or a service

This appears to be simple enough.

A product could be a drink, or a car, or a piece of clothing, something concrete which you can pay for and take away with you.

A service is something like a flight, a lawyer writing a will for you, a plumber fixing your leaks, a bus ride, or a museum visit.

Then again you might ask yourself, "What is Starbucks?" A product or a service? You get coffee which is definitely a product, but you also get a service and the experience of sitting in a café designed a bit like someone's living room. It doesn't matter as long as you appreciate that all this combined definitely makes up a brand.

A brand can also be a whole group of products or services. Cadbury (formerly known as Cadbury's) is a brand; so are Ford, Sony, BBC, HSBC, Olympus, Revlon, Burberry, The Gap, London Underground, Qantas, Vivienne Westwood, and Yamaha – one of my favorites because they make both excellent motorbikes and fantastic saxophones. Strange but true.

How about a film? Is *Star Wars* a brand? I'd say that it is, although each of the *Star Wars* films has made the overall brand feel slightly different. What about a person? Is Tom Cruise a brand? Were The Beatles a brand? I would say yes to both.

I deeply offended a monarchist by discussing Queen Elizabeth II's brand identity (and I meant the head of state in the United Kingdom not the cruise ship).

"She's not a brand; she's a person!" I was told. However, that would be to misunderstand exactly what a brand is. Anything or anyone which has a recognizable identity can be understood in terms of branding. When Napoleon Bonaparte had a statue of himself erected in the Place Vendôme in Paris, atop a massive column, dressed as Julius Caesar, what was he doing but building his brand identity amongst the Parisians?

Everyone with a publicist is actively building a brand of their own making including Her Royal Majesty. They try to control their bright, shiny, public images, but sometimes their actions conflict with the image to the point where the shine tarnishes. Product and service brands which associate themselves with personality brand images find that this can cut both ways. Did Madonna help The Gap or Jennifer Lopez help Louis Vuitton? How about Michael Jackson and Pepsi or David Beckham and his mobile phone?

Positioning

Professor Hankinson divided positioning into two parts: price – relative to the competition, and usage – what you actually do with it.

Describing price we use terms like down-market, mid-market or up-market. You might have a pricing policy which puts your brand at the top end of the mid-price bracket; essentially you are saying, "let's compare our prices with our rivals' and see where we fit." Marketers are taught that it is wrong to use nothing but its price to make a brand stand out from the rest because someone can always launch a brand with a higher or a lower price than yours and suddenly, if that's what you were relying on to make it look different, yours is nothing special. (Value is different. Value exists in the eyes of the beholder; it is an immensely subjective thing and we'll look into that later.)

Here's an example. Three of my favorite areas of interest, showing high, mid, and low priced brands:

Handbags	Chocolate	Perfume
Tanner Krolle	Charbonnel et Walker	Frederic Malle
Radley	Green & Black's	Cacharel
George at Asda	Aero	Body Shop

You can do the same with cars, computers, hotel groups, airlines; anything that has a price.

What do we mean by "usage" when we're talking about a brand? An example: what would you "use" yogurt for? Breakfast, dessert, a snack, a child's meal, a low-fat alternative to double cream on your strawberries?

You might think that usage is fairly obvious, but for marketers, it's worth investigating in case there is a "usage occasion" you haven't thought about. I worked with a man who "used" Mars bars for breakfast, lunch, and a snack to accompany his beer in the evening; after his first hospital trip he started to eat more fruit and vegetables. You might use a hotel for business but have you ever considered staying there at the weekend for fun? Perhaps you drive a Porsche for commuting, or for weekend breaks, for racing on track days, and taking the kids to see their grandmother.

When a brand owner suddenly spots a new usage opportunity we get advertisements which ask "Have you ever thought of ...?" or "Why not try it with ...?" suggesting that you put ice in your sherry and drink it instead of vodka and tonic, or that you use your fabric freshening spray on the dog's bed or in the car. When you spot those you can bet your last euro that someone just did a usage analysis to identify new ways to use their product more often. Jeans used to be workwear. White t-shirts were underwear until a young, muscular Marlon Brando took off his leather jacket to reveal on the silver screen that he had rebelliously left his shirt at home.

Personality

Professor Hankinson divides this into two, functional attributes and symbolic values – facts and feelings.

What if you were selling a rollerball pen, take one of my favorites, the Uniball Signo; how could we describe its functional attributes and symbolic values?

Functional attributes	Symbolic values
Japanese	Innovative
Wide range of colors:	Colors
standard	*fun*
pastel	*rare*
scented	*unusual*
sparkling	
Range of nib sizes	Reliable
Plastic	Classic design
Disposable	Classless

Functional attributes are things which everyone should agree about. They are facts.

It's the symbolic values on which everyone will have a different opinion, according to their own experience of the brand and what they've heard and read about it.

The more emotions a brand inspires, there more likely there are to be completely opposing views about it. The person responsible for marketing a brand attempts to control these views but it is a customer's own experiences – including advertisements and other marketing tools – which will form his or her own feelings about it.

If you were to list functional attributes for the BBC you might come up with:

- British
- television, radio, and Internet broadcaster
- mostly English language

- based in London, with regional and international operations.

Symbolic values are the things that make up a brand's image, whether it is cool or uncool, desirable or completely ignorable amongst a certain group of people.

People's views about the BBC might include:

- unbiased/biased
- establishment/radical
- populist/elitist/broad spectrum
- entertaining/boring
- reliable/unwatchable
- improving/dumbing down
- accessible/highbrow.

This is one of the biggest problems brand guardians have: when it comes to symbolic values everyone's views are different.

4
Separation may occur

Here is a definition from a US marketing book, *Marketing: relationships quality value:*

> Brand: a name, phrase, design, symbol, or a combination that identifies a product and differentiates it from rival products.[6]

This is saying is that you can forget completely about the quality of the product (or service) itself, and that all the brand is, is the name, strapline, or the logo. Take away the product and you've still got the brand? That's where, in my view, so many companies have lost the plot in recent years, starting to believe that a brand exists independently of the product or service is represents.

In 1999 Jane Yates of Interbrand Newell and Sorrell wrote:

> A brand is a name or a symbol – and its associated tangible and emotional attributes – that is intended to identify the goods or services of one seller in order to differentiate them from those of competitors. At the heart of a brand are trademark rights.[7]

I disagree; at the heart of a brand is the thing it was named after in the first place; the product or the service. It is not the name or the symbol that makes the difference – they are mere shorthand devices, even though they may have cost tens of thousands of dollars, pounds, euros, or yen to develop. If you were to change your name and change your clothes you'd still be you, wouldn't you? If you sold your name, your possessions, and your home would you have sold yourself? Of course not! If someone steals your identity are you still here?

Sometimes marketing directors get so caught up in defining a brand's image, they take their minds off the product itself, forgetting that the heart of the brand is not its symbolic values, but the thing that the customer really pays for. Once this happens, when the custodians of the brand fix their gaze on the image instead of the reality, then the counterfeiters can get a foothold.

Having said that, if a brand's identity is different according to your own experience of it, then perhaps your idea of a brand is different too. Who am I to judge Jane Yates, William G Nickels, and Marian Burk Wood? There I go, giving you a definition which I find useful, but you may think of a brand as something entirely different. Quite a few people who answered our research questionnaire understood "brand" to mean "luxury expensive designer name."

Here's Gareth Williams in *Branded? Products and their personalities:*

> What is a brand? A brand is a combination of names, slogans, product design, packaging, advertising and marketing that together give particular products or services a physical, recognisable form. But this is not all. Brands also have a cerebral dimension, which is the reputation they enjoy in the minds of customers. Brands must engender trust and loyalty if they are ultimately to be purchased. A brand, therefore, is a business strategy to encourage us to consume one product over its competitors, and it is a sign loaded with meaning that we choose to consume because we feel we related to it.[8]

Interesting.

In our research answers we got this answer: "I don't really wear brands. I just shop at Next in the UK."

Well, Next *is* a brand, according to me and the marketing school of thought, but if non-marketing people think that "brand = designer label" then perhaps marketers should think of a different term: time to rebrand the brand?

"Label" has become shorthand for "expensive clothing which you buy because it's got a recognizable name on it" rather than "a piece or bit of fabric with the manufacturer's name" on it and "brand" is heading that way too.

For practical reasons, I'll stick with Hankinson and Cowking.

Things beyond brand guardians' control can change symbolic values; these can damage sales. Sometimes, the brand guardians do it themselves when they make a daft decision. Perhaps they have hired one of the currently famous as a brand spokesperson then discovered that person turns out not to be an ideal representative of their values. In the case of Campari in the United Kingdom, a decision was made in the 1980s to increase sales by broadening the appeal; it was viewed as being an exclusive, European drink, rather too bitter for popular British taste. Actress Lorraine Chase, known for her down to earth, unpretentious attitude, was shown in a commercial drinking Campari with lemonade (which in the United Kingdom at that time was a very sweet fizzy drink which bore very little relation to lemons) opposite a sophisticated, suited European fellow drinking his with soda. Campari in the United Kingdom took quite a while to recover from the shock.

However, recover it did, and the reason it picked itself up and started again was that Campari is a drink whose functional attributes are strong. Brands' images can be nothing but fluff; mere ephemeral things which can be ruined at the drop of a headline. However, they will generally be open to ruin only if they are built on air, not on solid foundations. When a brand has had a great deal invested in its symbolic values but very little into sustaining its functional attributes it will not survive a crisis. If you deliver a good value product or service and never take your concentration away from its heart, you stand a fair chance of building a brand that endures.

5
Extension, stretching, and snapping

Taking a brand name and putting it on a different product or service used to be called brand stretching; this implied that there was some kind of hidden force pulling against the plan, so it metamorphosed into brand extension which makes it sound a lot less uncomfortable.

There is a belief in business that if your brand is strong and if enough people believe that it stands for "quality" – which is a moving target if ever there was one – that you can apply it to almost anything and your customers will buy whatever you put its name on.

I don't believe this, myself. When you forget what it was that earned that reputation in the first place, and start to construct a business on a brand's image then you are building your house on sand. Besides, companies can choose some awfully odd things to put their brand names on. Things which make you think, "They're selling WHAT?!" That's brand snapping.

Take Mont Blanc for example: they launched a fragrance. What should it smell of? Ink? For me, part of the Mont Blanc brand is the smell of Mont Blanc ink, which is a very wise brand extension if you happen to be best known for beautifully chunky fountain pens with a blob-of-snow logo on the cap. For those in the luxury product market, launching a fragrance is standard business practice now. It may turn out to be highly profitable.

To be fair, I went to visit the Mont Blanc shop in Bond Street, London W1 to smell the stuff. As a fan of writing in ink I was bowled over by the stunning pens they have there. A man was sitting at a writing desk, trying different nibs to make sure he bought the one which suited him best. Opposite was a sales assistant devoting her full attention to advising him. Mont Blanc is a major arts sponsor, which means that their customers are funding music, art, and writing. If you buy a Mont Blanc then you know that some of the profits are going towards this; if you would prefer a Bic Biro, then this is entirely up to you. The leather desk accessories seemed like a sensible move, as did the briefcases and the black and white handbags. The pen with its own heart-shaped red leather case and a bottle of red ink appealed to me most.

I was still not convinced by the fragrances; they are new-school, post-Eau d'Issey, interesting scents, but not a natural brand extension in my view, just one of those things everyone does once they have established a luxury brand identity.

Often brand extension works brilliantly, like Penguin Books selling branded pencils in sets of six classic Penguin paperback colors, Mr Muscle moving into floor cleaning cloths and Oxford University having its own Press.

Sometimes it doesn't; when I was teaching marketing at Hammersmith College I found it very odd that Rentokil, best known for their pest control, provided catering facilities at London educational establishments, as if the staff decided that they no longer wanted to be irritated by troublesome students. Doubtless Rentokil's expertise in ridding the capital of its rats and cockroaches meant that they had the business contacts to expand their operation into catering, but couldn't they have thought of another name? Rentokil is an established brand, which means that it already has a reputation but perhaps "Rentoserv" or similar would have been a little more appropriate?

In May 2004 Louis Vuitton Moët Hennessy (LVMH) bought Château d'Yquem, the sweet wine estate in Sauternes, known for its heritage, tradition, outstanding quality, and prices. Since Bernard Arnault took over LVMH, brand extensions have been the order of the day. Louis Vuitton itself has become a catwalk fashion brand, extending its reputation for handmade luggage which lasts a lifetime, into monogrammed jeans which last a season. Compte Alexandre Lur Saluces, the President of Yquem, found himself retired aged 70 after his family, including his children, voluntarily sold the majority of the shares in 1996. He had resisted for over a decade, hanging on to his share of the company his family had owned for 400 years. Reported in the UK's *Financial Times* one of his reasons was:

> Monsieur Arnault wants to make a perfume and call it d'Yquem. For 30 years I've fought against diluting the name of d'Yquem. Monsieur Arnault buys brands and does just about anything with them.[9]

However, he more recently stated, "Arnault understands that this is a jewel to be protected. I was wrong to suspect him." Bernard Arnault had appointed Lur Saluces as president of d'Yquen with control over winemaking, but not budgets.

After several decades of luxury brand extensions, with A-list actresses and singers launching their own eponymous perfumes, one could hardly blame the Count for his suspicions.

There is strongly held marketing view that it is much less risky to launch a product with a familiar name than a completely new one. If customers already know and trust a brand name, if trust is an appropriate word for a such a concept, then the theory is that they will be less timid about buying and trying the new thing.

So the Christian Dior, Chanel, Givenchy, and Yves Saint Laurent brands have been extended into accessories, perfume, and cosmetics, successfully making their products accessible (but not too accessible) to millions of people who can't afford the couture clothes while allowing those who can to match their current season's collection with their cosmetics. The accessories, cosmetics, and fragrance divisions are generally the profitable ones, but without the couture end the brands would be meaningless. As long as the designers (and the accountants) keep the couture innovative and healthy, then the extensions can thrive.

You·can buy Harley-Davidson motorcycle boots to go with your bike. This seems pretty sensible and so do the chrome polish to keep your exhaust pipes shiny and the leather luggage bags for you to put your overnight stuff in. You can also buy branded Harley-Davidson fragrance and fountain pens. Why on earth would anyone want to do that?

Marketers talk about strengthening or diluting their brand's identity. Imagine a brand's identity as a color painted on the boardroom wall. Let's use our imaginations and paint the Harley wall deep royal blue. If we decided to sell strong, well-made Harley branded boots, which are quite expensive as bike boots go, but will last you all your life (rather like the bike), we might allow ourselves to add an extra coat of royal blue paint to our wall. On the other hand, if we launched a bottle of Harley-Davidson fragrance it seems to me that we have to paint over our wall with a light shade of baby blue. Our dark blue still shows through but we've definitely lost a bit of its strength.

You could argue that Harley-Davidson lost the heart of its business when Mr. Harley and Mr. Davidson soldered their last rivet, but let's accept that as long as the organization makes decent bikes the brand's functional attributes remain intact. The shapes and styles of Harleys are widely and shamelessly copied by Japanese manufacturers, although they have never managed to synthesize the unmistakable clackety-clack of a Harley engine. However, although Harley is a luxury brand it's difficult to build a bike so it's pretty unlikely that you are ever going to find a completely counterfeit Harley-Davidson. (Having said that, there are counterfeit Honda scooters in China and the more I learn about the counterfeiting business, the less surprises me.)

As soon as a brand is extended into areas which commercialize its symbolic values its owners are practically sending out personalized invitations to counterfeiters to come in and copy. Anyone can make leather boots, belts, pens, and perfume cheaply then slap a label on them. If people buy a fake Harley product believing it to be real and it drops to bits, their experience will damage the brand's identity from their personal perspective – which is the only one they have. Harley have not painted over their dark blue; someone else has snatched the paintbrush, grabbed a pail of whitewash, and done it for them.

In the meantime, with every bottle of perfume and nail varnish they sell, Dior, Chanel, Givenchy, and YSL have been adding layer upon layer to their own deeply colored boardroom walls.

Talking of Harley, let's digress for a moment to take a look at the Von Dutch brand. Von Dutch was the nickname of Kenneth Howard, a substance abusing, people abusing racist who happened to have an outstanding talent for customizing vehicle bodywork, famous for his Harley-Davidson fuel tanks. Two views:

> While some custom car enthusiasts maintain that the line is disrespectful to the original Von Dutch, Caroline Rothwell, the company's Vice President of Marketing, believes the controversy gives the line an edge. "Von Dutch, the brand, is very organic, in that it actually comes from a true, untouched history," she says. "Many other clothing companies just don't have history to authenticate their brand name."[10]

> In the late 1960s, Von Dutch wrote off a car while under the influence. His wife, who was in the passenger seat, lost their unborn child. Von Dutch fled from California to Arizona to avoid being prosecuted for manslaughter.

> In the years that followed, Von Dutch became more violent and reclusive. By the time he died, he

was practically unapproachable, and was spending most of his time crafting and decorating guns. His last words were reportedly "Heil Hitler."[11]

With a history like that, perhaps a company would be better off with a brand name which wasn't quite so "authentic." Von Dutch Originals was set up to market the brand by people who never met Howard, and after a legal fight over the name with Howard's daughters the Von Dutch brand is now jointly owned. Their jeans cost around the $300 mark and you can buy sweet little pink and yellow Von Dutch kid's trainers for around $60. Oh, the irony!

On New York's Canal Street, home to every counterfeit fashion brand you could ever hope to encounter (and some very strange hybrids you've never heard of), Von Dutch fakes are sold openly to bunches of screeching schoolgirls who've seen Britney and Jason wearing their trucker hats and t-shirts. Von Dutch is a brand seemingly sent by the fashion gods for the counterfeiters to rip off to their heart's content. Its purchasers are not interested in the quality of the products, only in the logo. The dubious brand history is completely separate from the fashion goods stamped with the corporate identity and the message put out by the marketing team is that the brand is a bit edgy and wild. Wear Von Dutch and you are showing what a little rebel you really are. Buy a counterfeit Von Dutch and you're actually breaking the law! If people insist on throwing their money away there will always be someone happy to catch it.

But the fashion world itself may have the last word on Von Dutch Originals. Australian designer and fashion commentator Mandy Mills says: "People aren't interested in the quality of the product when they buy Von Dutch. It's all about a brand that they've been marketed into thinking they should wear. It doesn't represent anything. If anything, wearing it represents a lack of personality."[12]

In the meantime the directors of Von Dutch Originals are painting over the infamous flying eyeballs of their name-sake's artwork with a pretty shade of green which nicely matches the dollar bills they are raking in by the minute.

6
The promises brands make

Products only succeed because they consistently deliver the quality and value that their customers expect. If you buy a KitKat you want it to taste like the last KitKat you bought. You might buy it because you want to "have a break," as it says in the advertising, but if you were heading to the coffee shop for elevenses and you wanted to settle down with a hot drink and a quick chocolate biscuit you would be unlikely to buy a KitKat if you hadn't enjoyed your last one, no matter how many amusing ads you'd seen on television. We rely on the KitKat brand's integrity to keep the promise it makes to us. Likewise, if we go into a Starbucks in London we expect the coffee to taste the same as it does in Seattle or Sydney.

A counterfeit hijacks a brand's promises, delivering the superficial ones and breaking the rest. Whether or not this is important depends upon your point of view, and also whether a brand's promises are anything more than superficial. If you wanted a Burberry scarf because you know it's made from cashmere, so it's soft, warm, and durable, you will be disappointed when you buy the acrylic copy at a market stall. If you were buying it because you want the beige, red, white, and black check because you've seen someone wearing it in a "celebrity" gossip magazine, and you would like to buy into their image for a month or two, you get exactly what you want. You get "the look" which shows you are in touch with the world of fame and fortune. You get the symbolic values with only one of the physical attributes – the visual one.

What we think of brands depends on how we rate their performance and value. A brand's kudos can go up and down without the product varying in the slightest. Overnight a brand can become uncool, unfashionable, out of date, and unacceptable amongst a certain group of people, or it can go the other way. The Hush Puppy story is an interesting tale of a lost-in-the wilderness brand which was rescued by a small group of New Yorkers, used by Isaac Mizrahi in a catwalk show, and granted a reprieve amongst American shoe-buyers. Its rehabilitation was possible because the shoes were so well-made that they were sufficiently durable to be sought after in SoHo vintage clothing shops and still have a useful wearing life. If the "genuine Hush Puppies" the downtown dudes were searching for had dropped to bits after their first walk to the corner deli, they wouldn't have been rescued. (It would be fascinating to find the one person who made the first decision to wear an original pair; Hush Puppies should give him a medal.)

The point is that brand identity is held aloft by a scaffold of publicity but the foundations upon which it stands rely upon genuine quality and value.

Or, as Interbrand's chair Rita Clifton aptly put it:

> If brands are treated as a cosmetic oil slick on top of a pile of crap, then of course they're not going to work.[13]

Like beauty, quality and value exist in the eye of the beholder. We all see the value of a product according to our need or desire for it. I am content to pay more for a bottle of mineral water while sitting in the restaurant at the top of the Tate Modern, watching the sun go down over the London riverscape, drinking from a glass I don't have to wash, served by a pleasant person wearing a t-shirt which matches the painting on the back wall, than I would for one at the local shop. There are people who would never in a million years agree to fork out four times the shop price of water for the Tate Modern version. I've watched them pointedly ask for tap water because it's "free" and they wish to make it clear that they should not be expected to pay for it. (It is convenient to forget about the overheads we are adding to while we are borrowing their glasses, sitting on their chairs, being lit by their electricity, being served by their waiters.) Our experiences shape our perceptions which shape our opinions of brands and everything else in our lives. I believe that the Tate Modern café should make a profit which goes towards running the gallery, that I should contribute to the running costs and that this makes water expensive. Others are of the view that a state-owned gallery should provide free water for its visitors. I believe they should drink from a paper cup filled from the drinking fountain. In this case we all have a choice.

However, with many luxury brands most people do not have the choice of whether to buy them or not. Is a Chanel lipstick costing 20 euros a luxury item? It is a luxury lipstick, but it is not totally inaccessible to most of the people who would ever consider buying a lipstick. It may be 20 times more expensive than a cheap one, but in our consumer society it could be saved for or splashed out on or put on a credit card and worried about later. With a luxury watch or bag the position changes; a copy may cost $50, but the one it is imitating costs $600. What do we do if we want one? We have seen the advertisements, read about it in magazines, seen a paparazzo shot of a film star carrying one, and the more we think about it, the more we desire it. Do we save up? Do we dismiss the very thought and say to ourselves, "Don't be silly. If I ever had $600 to spend on a watch, I would spend it on a new washer-dryer!" Do we put it on our credit cards and worry about it later? Or do we buy a fake one?

The luxury one has been manufactured from the finest materials, assembled by hand and tested for durability. If something goes wrong it will be replaced or repaired. The designer is financially rewarded, the manufacturer's share-holders expect a dividend this year, the company sponsors a technological marvel of a yacht in a round-the-world race, and the managing director travels the world in the group's private jet. The fake has been copied, probably from an

Internet image; the bindings will tarnish, it may drop to bits, it was assembled at a Chinese factory which may not have adequate facilities for its workers, it may have been imported by organized crime gangs as a means of laundering drug money, and if something goes wrong you will never be able to find the person who sold it to you.

The reason that fakes can swoop in and swipe business from under a brand's nose is that purchasers can convince themselves that they are buying just enough of that brand's prestige to make it worthwhile. They know they aren't getting it all – that's why the fake is cheaper – but they are getting some of it, sufficient to make it desirable.

But would a person who will buy the counterfeit version ever have bought the real thing? Or vice versa? The official view is that counterfeiters steal business from genuine brands. It is without question that they steal the ideas and the intellectual property, but do they earn money which the luxury brands would have earned for themselves? Would a person who is prepared to spend the money on a $2000 bag, spend it instead on a $200 fake? According to our research, as a general rule, no, but as the quality of counterfeits is increasing, the general rule seems to be changing.

We assume that our senior colleagues, our wealthier relations, or the smartly dressed people we see in the street are carrying the genuine branded goods. In the United States, if not the rest of the world, our collected anecdotal evidence suggests that more and more are economizing on their handbags and buying fakes. They may be dressed head to toe in Prada, but now that scarcely anyone can tell the difference between a top-end Chinese counterfeit and the real thing, more American women are letting their inner budgets speak louder than their inner lawyer and buying the fake. Many trade up after buying fakes; having developed a taste for the look, they hanker for the real thing. But some are trading down again because they simply cannot see the point of paying ten times more for what looks and feels like the genuine article. The buying experience may have an influence. You have to have courage to open the door and step inside some of those luxury brand boutiques. If you aren't wearing the right shoes you can be frozen ice-cold with one glance from a discerning (or discriminating) sales assistant. Personally, I'd always rather buy luxury goods from friendly assistants at Heathrow Airport than in Bond Street shops. I know where I'm not welcome and frankly I'll never be posh enough to cut the mustard in London W1. Maybe they reckon I would damage their brand if I were seen out and about with their bags.

The US trade in "purse parties" (like Tupperware parties except with counterfeit designer bags for sale) was recently clamped down upon by police and customs in Miami. Groups of well-heeled ladies were meeting to buy and sell their bargain fakes, choosing to ignore any unpleasant illegalities. These purses are smuggled into the country evading taxes, probably imported by criminal gangs, and definitely breaking intellectual property law, but are they taking business from the real thing? Would the ladies have bought genuine Kate Spade? Will they do so now their supplies of the fake stuff have been cut off?

Often it is not the counterfeits, but the legal copies that take away business from the innovative brands. The Body Shop lost approximately 25 percent of its UK sales in one year when Boots launched its "Natural Collection" and this almost took down the entire business. At the Musée de la Contrefaçon, next to a genuine Perrier bottle, there is a range of other sparkling mineral waters, recognized brands, all in pear-shaped green glass bottles. Perrier considers that every one of these is an infringement of its intellectual property rights. Highland Spring, the Scottish water, is one of the brands on display clearly labeled as a Perrier copy. Highland Spring, available on supermarket shelves beside Perrier throughout the world, is much more likely to take its sales than a truck load of "Pellier" water, sourced from a tap somewhere, carbonated and sold on the black market. Perrier considers its imitators to be trading off its own good reputation.

For those people who are fortunate enough to have a choice between the genuine brand and a counterfeit, which will people choose? It depends how much the symbolic values matter more than the functional attributes, what their social group does, and whether or not they think anyone will notice.

7
Real stories about fakes

There seems to be something paradoxically pleasing about misleading people into thinking you've spent a lot of money when you haven't. It exposes those who measure success by the height of their pile of cash.

Here are some short shopping stories:[14]

> One of my friends wanted a fake LV bag as a present. If feels as though you are thumbing your nose at people who are stupid enough to waste thousands of pounds on a handbag.

> [I] purchased [a purse] in Canal Street market in New York, all fake brands openly on sale in market stalls with mainly oriental vendors... 'there was no suggestion at all that they were real. The price = cheap. Looked good and stylish.

> I bought a purple-fake-snake-skin-Gucci-y-hand-bag outside Russell Square tube once. It wasn't officially fake. I just liked it for its obvious plastic-ness and wore it to a posh concert, to mock the overpriced bags people tend to take there, It was just 5 pounds and the last one in the stall!

> I once bought a fake Chanel backpack for $24 (haggled down from $40) on a street corner in mid-town Manhattan, NYC. Vendor only sold bags. His English wasn't that great, but I believe both he and I started with the understanding that these were not the real deal. The bag had a wonderful shape and design to it that I had not seen before and it greatly appealed to me. I wore it for close to 5 years almost daily before it fell apart and I replaced it with a different brand but with a close enough similarity to size and shape.

Our research asked respondents what they thought was the difference between genuine brands and counterfeit goods. Of the respondents 78 percent used the word "quality" and others mentioned "attention to detail" and "materials and manufacture." Only eight out of 46 mentioned ethics and morality; six of those thought that counterfeit brands were immoral and two came out against the genuine but expensive brands.

> The amount of profit made – some of the luxury brands this is insane. The quality of the time and the amount people are paid to make them do not justify the cost. The money is used to pay for advertising and to subsidise the haute couture ends of the business.

The alternative view:

> I think that real clothes and accessories are made by people who wear them and use them; fake clothes are what designers try and sell at extortionate prices to people who want to buy them to look trendy and hip in order to be accepted and feel pride in themselves!

Those against counterfeits said they thought the difference was:

> Quality of merchandise and a sense of personal morality.

> The quality of the materials. The question of who gets my hard-earned dosh in their pockets is more worrying to me.

> I think the quality of materials used, the amount of money workers were paid for their labour, the

legitimacy of where the money is going, and the accountability if something goes wrong.

I have seen fake perfumes, handbags etc. in the market. As least I assume they are fakes on account of the unlikely low prices. Either that or they are stolen (and in my eyes that's a pretty fine line anyway).

The quality is a big difference between real and fake stuff. Imitations are usually very cheap. I like to wear clothes that are real even if I have to get them at sales or through discounts, mainly because I feel imitations cheat the designer/company. I felt so bad about buying the fake bag I never used it and later gave it away.

Fake brand is a thief.

There is a beautiful expression which is used to legitimize fakes, "faux-designer;" the French for fake seems more elegant and sophisticated. "Authentic replica" is another splendid euphemism rolled out to make counterfeits seem less illegal.

However, most of our respondents seemed unaffected by the legality or ethics of the fakes business. For them it was a simple question of whether the goods appealed or not. They might be low quality but then probably so was the merchandise on the market stall next to it; no real difference between low quality fakes and low quality unbranded goods.

Some even came out in favor of buying counterfeits:

Knock-offs can be good to have if you take them in that vein. Some are gorgeous and if they're well made and don't cost a lot, why not?

Some were distinctive only for their ambivalence:

> Depends on the manufacturer. With "good" fakes, the only difference you'll notice is the price. Others have shoddy quality – bad seamwork, unusual fit, low-quality dyes, using a print instead of the actual weave, that kind of thing.

> The price ... I'd say sometimes quality, but sometimes the quality is as good.

> I really have no problem buying fakes, even though I've never done so (never had the opportunity), they will obviously be lesser in quality to the name brands, but those name brands are quite expensive.

> Quality used to be the difference but these days you can get fakes that really look like they came out of the same factory. If they are run-ons are they fakes or not? How do we tell these days? Is a hologram label any different than having a receipt that says you paid a certain amount for a product?

> The differences are in the quality and emotional satisfaction. Some fakes are so good that they can be as good as the real thing ... and of course you don't get the feeling of being ripped off yet you don't get the same level satisfaction from buying a fake.

So this person ambivalently feels that luxury goods are a rip-off, but that counterfeits somehow disappoint the purchaser. For some, the majority, the goods are assessed purely on value:

I don't have a problem with fakes as long as they are good quality.

Quality and price ... in a way, you get what you pay for, with fakes being of very poor quality and status products being way over priced.

Quality of materials and workmanship. And the brand name, if it matters to you.

Fake articles are lower quality (boyfriend bought a "Rolex" watch as a gift that stopped working the next day), but obviously cheaper.

I've never had any desire to buy fake designer goods, not because of any moral compunction, but because I think they're poorly made, they're ugly and that everyone will know they're fakes anyway, as I certainly can't afford designer bags, etc.

Quality, but sometimes there is not much different beside the price and the buying experience.

A sample size of 53 people, of whom 46 answered the question, is quite a small number from which to draw conclusions about the whole market. However it's about the same size as eight focus groups, and a lot of opinions have been based on those in the past – so even if it doesn't represent the views of the entire market, it gives us food for thought.

The conclusion from the evidence collected is that the CIA, Interpol, the Union des Fabricants, and the various anti-counterfeiting organizations worldwide have yet to make their points sufficiently strongly. The view that creative people deserve to make profits from their creativity seems to fade to irrelevance when it comes to luxury brands which are judged to make massive profits at the expense of silly people who will pay over the odds in order to impress other silly people. When a luxury manufacturer hires a bulldozer to destroy thousands of fakes in a show of publicity, common sense comes storming out to protest against the wasteful profligacy of these upper-class vandals. Making an example of the watches, rather than the people behind the illegal manufacture, smuggling, and profiting from fakes, seems a bit ludicrous. We just feel sorry for the watches.

When Louis Vuitton and Hermès bags are copied, or you can buy a fake Cartier watch for $20, the general feeling is that the accountants who run designer labels these days won't miss the odd dollar in the coffers as they are already raking it in. There is often more sympathy with the person selling the goods, seen as "the little guy" being oppressed by big business.

This is frequently the view of the legal system beyond the borders of the wealthier countries. Even in Italy, which is believed to be top of the grubby heap of European counterfeiters, judges have a habit of siding with a local company which is making counterfeits, over the brand's owner. According to my Italian chum Marco, an Italian court prosecuted one of the many men who come in by train then settle down for the afternoon and evening, spreading out their counterfeit bags on the pavements of Venice. The offence was "passing off" – he was charged with a trademark infringement, pretending that his counterfeit goods were the real deal by having the logo all over them – but the judge let him off because he said that at one tenth the price of the real bag, only an idiot would believe she was buying the real thing from a man sitting on the pavement; the vendor would only be "passing them off" as genuine goods if he were charging more money. Case dismissed. This doesn't seem quite fair. If I were the person having my designs copied, I would be furious about that, but where intellectual property law is concerned, things are complicated.

Observations from Rouse & Co. International, IP lawyers:

> In cases of relatively non technical goods such as apparel, IP holders can run into difficulties when giving evidence that particular items are counterfeit. Counterfeiting cases are heard by the Magistrates courts, where judges may not be very IP savvy. On occasions good defense counsel have put identification experts on the spot, and raised a reasonable doubt about their ability to identify fake goods with 100 percent accuracy. This, even where the goods are plainly counterfeit.
>
> To counter this risk, IP holders need to use markings, labeling, covert identification technologies to ensure accurate identification. In addition they need to have tight distribution chains, properly controlled with contracts and inspections to ensure parallel goods and overruns do not appear so the leaks are plugged as soon as they are discovered. In such cases IP holders will be more confident about giving evidence that an item is fake. Witnesses also need to understand the process of cross examination and the issue of reasonable doubt, before giving evidence.[15]

The view from each country is different. One view is that the West is trying to take over the world with its materialist, decadent values:

> Happiness in a dishwasher, social status in an automobile, beauty in a bottle of hair colour. These are the goods and values the West is ostensibly offering the rest of the world. These are the goods and values which, in the minds of many critics of the consumer society, have already brought the West to a state of moral and social decay.[16]

Copies of Western goods exist all over the world. The imitators probably feel very differently about them than the imitated. Why shouldn't a small, local manufacturer imitate a Western multinational and employ his neighbors to make and distribute his own goods to local retailers, instead of importing them from the West? Often the local legal system supports the local market:

> In the 1960s, a merchant in Mexico City named Fernando Pelletier opened a shop called "Cartier" and started selling precise imitations of goods – watches, leather goods, pens – produced by the French company of the same name, at discount prices. When it discovered that its goods were being counterfeited, the original Cartier company decided to open its own shop in Mexico. The Mexican Cartier, in response, sent a letter to the President of Mexico denouncing the French Cartier's lack of respect for Mexican industry and government, and suggesting that the French products were fakes. This letter was printed in major Mexican newspapers and soon became the subject of angry editorials against the French invaders. The French Cartier also ran into problems when it tried to register its trademark designs in Mexico, for it found that Pelletier had already registered them and had thus prior rights to them.
>
> Eventually in 1981, Pelletier – by then a millionaire – made the mistake of travelling to France where he was arrested for counterfeiting. In exchange for his release, and the rights to become one of Cartier's authorized agents in Mexico, Pelletier agreed to stop using the Cartier name for his own products.[17]

The case for small local companies copying Western goods for their own market is explained by Jonathan Fenby:

> If people want jeans that look like Levis, and local workshops can turn out a reasonable imitation, why spend much-needed hard currency on importing the real thing? The only sufferer is a distant firm with a famous name which can easily be dismissed as a rich multinational that doesn't need the money and is probably exploiting Third World markets in any case.[18]

Much has changed since Jonathan Fenby wrote that in 1983. Copying and counterfeiting are creating exploitative multinationals of their own, making immense illegal, untaxed profits, some of which are used to fund drug trafficking, prostitution, and terrorism. Customers tend to ignore that side, when all they want is a cheap handbag with an expensive logo on it.

Reading reports about Japan, we could get the impression that women are so obsessed with Western luxury brands that they would sell their grandmothers to get the latest Louis Vuitton bag. It is perfectly true that there are a fair few Louis Vuitton bags around. One Japanese chum told me that she thinks it looks rather silly to have only the bag and not the rest of the outfit. In her opinion French or Italian women would buy a luxury handbag to accessorize their beautifully designed and crafted clothes, not to wear as a badge to the office each day, matched with a plain gray suit, white socks, and chunky black shoes.

What about fakes? The Japanese don't buy them, at least not any more. Jonathan Fenby's book tells the tale of a Hermès tie which Emperor Hirohito thought he was wearing for a photo-shoot. It had been bought from a reputable Tokyo department store, but it was a counterfeit.

Japan has cleaned up its act to the point of spotlessness since then. A young female Japanese office worker or the wife of a businessman, the classic target markets for luxury Western brands, would not consider buying a counterfeit. The term for the young, female office workers is "OL," pronounced "oeru," an abbreviation of Japanese–English Office Lady. They commute in their hundreds of thousands to Tokyo daily. My Japanese chum and marketing manager, Sae, told me:

> These days "OL" is left unused, because it sounds a little sexist word. But nowadays fashion magazine uses it like nickname. So everyone knows this word. You know, OLs are an enthusiast of European brand like Louis Vuitton, Gucci, Prada, and Fendi etc.

On a brief visit to Tokyo and Yokohama, I went looking for luxury brands and their counterpart counterfeits to see if there really were none at all. I was relieved to find that even here in squeaky-clean Japan, at a mid-market shopping mall, there were a few copies of Burberry scarves. However, there were many more real ones, notably worn by uniformed school girls traveling home on the train, carefully tied so that the labels faced outwards; the favored color scheme was the navy blue check, not the ubiquitous beige. Some copycat brands existed, as the Japanese love to use Western (usually English) writing on their products. There was a BBC Shop, using the same logo style as the international broadcaster, but selling clothes, not DVDs of British television programs. There were copies of Gucci and Dior-style bags with monograms woven into their fabric. My favorite brand of those inspired by European luxury goods was Miss Pinky, a decorative range of mid-market bags designed in the style of Paris and Milan's most opulent extravagances.

However, not even in Yokohama's Chinatown will you find a hint of a counterfeit. One reason is that the Japanese are generally much more law abiding than Americans and Europeans. There is very little crime. It is not a matter of choice whether or not to buy an illegal product; now it is simply unacceptable. The fascinating alternative is the booming Japanese "recycle" market. At newsagents you can buy the Japanese Chanel, Gucci, Vuitton, Hermès, and Bulgari catalogs, published by Kotsu Times; you can buy mini versions to carry around in your Chanel, Gucci, Vuitton, or Hermès handbag. You can also buy thick, glossy magazines full of ads for second-hand luxury branded goods. The shops advertised are as smart as designer boutiques, the bags are in perfect condition, and the companies that deal in them are large enough to be stock market listed.

Hong Kong has a similar market for second-hand luxury brands amongst the Chinese residents, but not the European and American visitors.

"Only the tourists buy fakes," said my Hong Kong chum Tiffany, who lugs her Louis Vuitton monogram business bag wherever she goes.

"Are they made in Hong Kong?" I asked.

"Not any more. They come from Korea," she said.

"It may be Korean businessmen who import them," said Alex, a genial entrepreneur from Taiwan, "but they have them made in China. No one can compete with the Chinese on price these days."

My prediction is that there will not be a market for counterfeits in Japan in the near future; Japanese customers are simply not interested and their desire for luxury brands shows no sign of wearing out. Their creativity is flourishing and Japanese luxury brands are on the rise to challenge European ones. Japan is not immune to the trade in counterfeits. Customs have stopped shipments on their way into and out of the country, and as the quality of the copies increases, it's possible that some fake bags might sneak in and be sold as the real thing, but my view is that deliberately setting out to buy fakes is not on the OLs' agenda. They want to buy the whole brand package, including the quality and the price tag.

American and European luxury brand owners have managed, in a few decades, to cultivate brand loyalty in the Far East, which borders on obsession. At the same time they have lost much of the loyalty amongst their native markets to Chinese manufacturers via less than scrupulous importers to customers who no longer feel that the quality justifies the prices.

8
Brand loyalty: Why do we feel affection for a "thing"?

Do we really love brands as is claimed on the front page of this very book; if so, why? And when I say "we love brands but buy fakes" it might not be you and I who buy the fakes, but at 7 percent of world trade billions of people do. Perhaps we've bought some and not even known about it.

My friend Patrick, a barrister who has strong opinions on everything and loves a good argument, says that there is only a market for pirated films on DVD because the public has decided that they are not worth what the shops are charging. He reckons that the law trails miles behind the reality and shows no signs of catching up. He also believes that luxury brand identity is all a load of codswallop and that there is no reason to buy a hugely expensive, well-made handbag which will go out of fashion in a season when you could have a cheap one which looks just like it and will last just long enough to be replaced by the new model from the next season.

Then again, Patrick doesn't buy handbags. He probably doesn't feel that way about suits, leather brogues, or briefcases.

What marketers call "brand loyalty" was described by the UK head of *Readers' Digest*, Henry van Wyck as: "What's left when you take away all the bribes."[19]

What he meant was that if you stop discounting, running competitions, giving two for the price of one offers, and call a halt to all the other promotional tools, and your customers still choose your brands that is how you can tell that they feel loyal. If a rival tried to steal them away from you by discounting, running competitions, and doing all the things you used to do, would they go? If they stay with you, you have earned their brand loyalty.

We all have our favorites, the ones we rely on. Often we can be tempted to try an alternative especially if it's cheaper, but it's not usually price which wins our loyalty; it is whether we feel that the quality of the product or service matches the price and if our whole experience involved in buying it gave us a good feeling or a bad one. You may have eaten a marvelous meal in a beautiful restaurant, but if the staff were rude to you, would you go back? Would you rather go somewhere the food isn't quite so splendid but the people are welcoming? But if the food is bad, someone will have to present a very strong argument to get you back there.

I buy innocent brand smoothies, lovely juices, and fruity waters. They cost more than other people's fresh drinks, especially the ones that are presented in copycat packaging as supermarket own brands, but I like innocent, I just do. I've met some of the people who work there; I like what they write on their bottles and I love the drinks. I particularly like the way that they can give me my five helpings of fruit all in one smoothie with hardly any effort on my part. I consider myself to be a pretty loyal customer of theirs.

I am loyal to Waitrose for grocery shopping, Liberty for clothes and afternoon tea with my friends, Lush for skincare and haircare (and not just because I write for them), Canon and Lomo for cameras, Smythson and Paperchase for stationery, *Eve* magazine, the *Harvard Business Review*, the *Observer* Sunday newspaper, Snappy Snaps in Ealing Broadway, Lancôme Juicy Tubes, British Airways, Green and Black's chocolate, B. K. S. Iyengar's method of yoga, Bunker Optician's in Henley-on-Thames. (Forgive the British bias, but I live here.)

What are yours?

Do you ever find yourself feeling vaguely guilty because you have bought a different brand from your favorite? That is brand loyalty taking hold.

Sometimes we stay loyal out of convenience, ease, familiarity, or laziness. The majority of people only change brands because someone involved has been rude to them, or they have been made to feel uncomfortable. Sometimes lost customers can be tempted back with a genuine apology and a desire to make up for the insult, whether it was intentional or accidental. When this happens they can end up more loyal than ever, because the organization has really made an effort to show it cares – but that's a whole different book.

In my experience, loyal customers swarm around products and services which are so good that the company's employees use them and buy them for their friends and family too – if they can afford them – and would have no hesitation in recommending them to others, even after they moved jobs. If you find yourself working for an organization whose products you would not recommend to your best mate, leave. If your organization is about to launch something which you know to be useless, quit. If we all do it, then rubbish brands will cease to exist. If we hang on in there hoping for promotion and not wanting to upset the boss, useless brands will continue to be launched, offering massive "consumer choice" but restricting our ability to find what we want.

Brand loyalty is found where customers find both quality and value.

9
What you say and what I hear

Quality can exist simultaneously with a bad brand identity if the symbolic values have been neglected while the brand guardians concentrate on the physical attributes alone. When that happens they are undefended against criticism, sometimes from rival brands. It all depends on customers' individual experiences. An example: I have a good friend called Bill. He runs marathons in very respectable times, lives in a small town in Yorkshire, currently works in the probation service but was happiest when he was a postman in the Yorkshire Dales. He visits me in London for a bit of peace and quiet. "What?" say his friends, "London? For peace and quiet?" They picture Oxford Street and the tourist bits and expect it to be bustling, busy, and exhausting. However, they don't know my little part of London, a 1930s complex of 132 apartments with our own garden and a mini-lido. For starters, there are two different versions of Brand London, and I've not yet reached the point of the story.

Our favorite little coffee shop, Spill the Beans, closed down when the owner sold up to live in Italy with his Italian wife and their small children. Incidentally, Spill the Beans had not closed down because the big ones moved in and forced him to close; in fact he had been doing marvelously, so well that he had bought himself a beautiful plot and large home which he was intending to run it a yoga center and retreat; he just got tired of working long hours, getting up in the morning in time for the pre-office rush. My brand new favorite coffee shop is Kavah, an Internet café with leather sofas, a pleasant, south-facing back garden, and good cakes, but it hadn't yet opened last time Bill was staying; the available options were Coffee Republic, Starbucks, and Costa Coffee.

"I won't go in Starbucks," said Bill.

"Don't you like the taste?" I asked him.

"I've never tried it," he said. "I've read all about them being multinationalist, globalising the world and serving crap coffee."

I took him to Starbucks. Once you are there you can read about how Starbucks do not use Robusta beans, the ones which campaigners rightly object to as their growers are often exploited by large companies; they use Arabica beans which are more expensive but grown in better conditions.

Bill had a caffe latte and he was knocked out to find that it tasted good.

You can't blame campaigners for campaigning and many times they have been proved right. Cigarette manufacturers denied for years that smoking was detrimental to health, deliberately concealing evidence to the contrary. 100 percent pure beef turned out to mean 100 percent of the entire cow, including the bits that we don't want to think about. We can be just as easily influenced by non-commercial organizations as by commercial ones. Given past records of corporate economy with the truth, these days media-savvy individuals are sometimes more skeptical about the genuine truths manufacturers tell, but eager to latch on to slanderous tales of cheating, poisoning, bad working practice, and carcinogenic chemicals without checking the facts first.

Sometimes well-intentioned campaigners are fed duff material by people with an axe to grind, including rival manufacturers. This happens all the time in the cosmetics industry. Just last night I was harangued yet again by a well-intentioned acquaintance about how Lush's shampoo should be made without preservative – actually, an untreated liquid shampoo made without preservative would go moldy in weeks – unaware that her own favorite "green" brand is irradiated to stop it going off. Insufficient information can light a short fuse.

On the Lush cosmetics customer forum (North American version) I read a well-argued proposition stating that the reason Lush Fresh Handmade Cosmetics does not open shops at a faster rate in the United States is that the company is deliberately restricting demand in order to create a buzz about the products, get people talking, and create unsatisfied desires. In this way when shops do finally open, she explained, Lush would have a ready made instant market desperate to buy the products. She knew this, she said, because her sister was studying for her MBA at Harvard and she had investigated Lush's strategy. What she could have done was asked Lush. The facts are that the shop team is looking for good locations around the world all the time; when they find a perfect place 99 percent of the time a company with more money outbids them. It took six years to find a decent site in Paris. Lush is actually quite a small, private company so expansion is funded from profits. The reason the products are talked about is because they are well made and good value. It all sounds a bit old-fashioned and so it is; that is not necessarily a bad thing. Instead of sitting in their corporate HQs devising hype strategies to excite their customers, perhaps some of the MBA postgraduates should just make better value products.

While we are on the subject of misunderstanding, the word "natural" is having a crisis too. In cosmetics, it is used to mean "sourced directly from nature" but also used to imply gentle, mild, safe, and kind for the skin. Opium is natural, so are poison ivy, belladonna, cocaine, and wasps. The word has been appropriated by every air freshener, fabric conditioner, washing powder, body lotion, and soap to mean something along the lines of "full of the joys of spring with flowers and fluffy bunnies everywhere." In other words, when you read "natural" on a piece of packaging it no longer means anything at all. Mother Nature doesn't have any brand guardians to fight back and place appropriate features in the media.

Unilever got into trouble in Sweden for their ice cream. A lolly called 88 has been bought to the attention of the Anti-Discrimination Bureau in Malmo "on the grounds that 88 is a neo-Nazi code for Heil Hitler."[20] Their Walls brand has a logo devised from the word "Walls" formed into a heart shape. Apparently, if you turn it upside down and squint, it looks like the word *Allah* in Arabic, so the design has had to be changed. I would bet large amounts of money that neither of these were intentional or even dreamed of in their worst nightmares, when Unilever's brand guardians were designing their communications strategies.

The brands people choose to use say things about them, but what they are saying depends on who is listening. When they notice a woman carrying the newest Louis Vuitton, Marc Jacobs, Takashi Murakami monogram bag, what do you imagine people think?

"That woman's got a pretty bag." (That's my mum and most of the rest of the world to whom Louis Vuitton means about as much as whoever has topped the Latvian singles charts this week. (No offence to the Latvian music industry intended.))

"That woman is filthy rich." (Someone who would love one just like it but doesn't have the money.)

"That woman has style and good taste." (Someone who already owns one.)

"That woman belongs to a world I would love to join." (Intends to seduce someone who can afford to buy one for her.)

"That woman is daft enough to spend $2000 on a bag!" (Someone who intends to buy a counterfeit.)

"I've got one just like that." (Someone who already bought a counterfeit.)

"That woman must hang out with some really empty-headed people."

"That woman must be very insecure if her self-image depends upon expensive accessories."

"That woman doesn't look as if she could afford a real one of those bags so she must be a saddo who buys fakes."

"That woman is mightily pretentious."

What about someone who has just bought a counterfeit copy of the same thing? Depending on how good a rip-off it was and how much time the observer spends reading fashion magazines, they could think any of the above or, as Marietta Pacella puts it:

> That women "looks like a yobbo and merely has a destined-to-fall-apart accessory that makes her look like a superficial phony who seems to believe that one can buy respect or importance via a name brand."[21]

Do we care what other people think? Weather and practicality notwithstanding, would we wear the same clothes if we were staying in or going out? What if we were going out with the friends we see every week as opposed to going to a school reunion? Meeting the bank manager or meeting the tax inspector?

During his one-man show the late Quentin Crisp, who created his own style and resolutely refused to adopt one the slightest bit like anyone else's, told audiences that one was not being rebellious if the style of one's group was to rebel. If a group consisted of punks who liked to pierce their ears with safely pins and chain their trouser legs together, then a true rebel would wear tweeds, a twin set, and pearls. He also said that one should never wear a hat with more personality than oneself.

We may dispute that we care what anyone thinks about us, who we are, what we do, the way we dress, and what we spend our money on, but apart from a few rare individuals like Eastern holy men and philosophers with no time for superficial thoughts, the rest of us humdrum humans do value the opinions of those we like and admire.

Life gets tricky for the insecure who value the opinions of

almost everyone above their own. A friend of mine once brought round an outfit she was planning to wear for a wedding. "I'm a bit worried," she said, "because Marie (her neighbor) doesn't like it."

"But Marie is an idiot, isn't she?" I said. "And you've never admired her taste in clothes."

"Oh yes," said my chum, "So that's OK then."

From our research, here are some views on brands that people would prefer not to buy, which their guardians may not be expecting:

> I would carry a brown paper sack before I'd carry a big, flashy Louis Vuitton bag, just because I think that it screams, "Look at me! I want everyone to know/think I'm wealthy!"

> I would never wear clothes made by Jennifer Lopez, Ecko Red, or Baby Phat. For some reason they seem trashy and flashy to me.

> I can't think of any brands, per se, but you won't see me wearing ANY label or logo on the outside of my clothing.

> Von Dutch, Juicy Couture, Burberry (unless it's a pink Burberry umbrella, cos they're kind of cute) because every trendy girl wears them proudly with the labels showing. That gets on my nerves.

> I don't like things that scream "look at me I am xxxxx brand" so I will never own a Louis Vuitton purse. I wouldn't buy something just because of who makes it or because it makes me "cool" to have it. I'd probably never wear Versace, because I think it tends to look tacky.

D&G – too colorful.

Jordache jeans, because for me they have too many associations with skanky 80s tight jeans and far too much stonewash.

I think Lacoste where I am is so fashionable it's ridiculous. So I'd probably refuse to wear it for that reason.

Designer clothes with obvious logos splashed all over them (such as a Louis Vuitton handbag, for example). Don't like status symbol clothing that shows off how much you have spent on something.

Big designer brands. I just don't ascribe to the whole lifestyle associated with them.

Sag Harbor – the name is off-putting.

I will not purchase anything at Wal-Mart because it is bad for communities. Otherwise I'm not that brand conscious I make my decisions more based on style. I do avoid choosing some items at GAP because you will run into at least two people a week wearing an item that you have and everybody knows that you bought it at GAP.

Gucci, Versace … I wouldn't wear a label if I knew they used fur in their collections.

Louis Vuitton bags. I really dislike anything that has to have its initials everywhere on the product. And the concept of putting people on waiting lists is just darn ridiculous.

Christian Dior (not now that Galliano has taken over. Sure, he's creative, but unless you want to pay top dollar for an item that will last you only one season ... well, otherwise, instead of a chic derelict, you wind up looking like an out-of-date derelict. Both are crap options in my opinion. His clothes are best seen on his humorously created caricatures on the runway, not in everyday life.) Plus, all this "J'adore Dior" crap with the logos all over it.... I'm not into paying big money to give LVMH free advertising just so people can say "Oh look at her. She's wearing a Dior." Anyone who is impressed by WHO I am wearing over WHAT I am wearing has their priorities completely botched.

And Prada, generally. I'm not big on looking like a relatively stylish, retirement age school marm from the 40s.

Oh, and Moschino. Looks like junk with a big-name brand attached to it. Plus, they often try too hard to cater to the young, and even then, they're fairly out of touch in my opinion. It's like they can't decide between girlie and conservative or masculine and daring, so they throw all of the above into one piece. Basically, they offer nothing but painful sensory overload.

I'm wondering if I am the right person for this questionnaire. I have no shame. I just bought a jacket, slippers and pyjamas in Primark. Bargain.

FCUK with the logo splashed all over it. I'd rather chew off my own leg than wear FCUK.

Anyone under the impression that modern consumers blindly follow trends and have no opinions of their own will be reassured by those honest views. The brand's owners probably won't worry too much as they have a willing market of label-ravenous consumers ready to join their waiting lists, in order to confirm the apparent exclusivity of their own existences. However, bearing in mind what happened to Burberry when it became just at little over-visual in the United Kingdom, it may not do to dismiss these views completely.

10
Brands and their logos

There's a converted pub on the corner of Marylebone High Street and Paddington Street, London W1. From the window you can see a road sign; it points left and has a blue background with a P on it. It is of course the multinational sign for a public car park, showing that this one is off the left-hand side of the street. Brand guardians long for an instantly recognizable identity like that; their owners invest much money creating signs which they hope will convey as much information with such little effort.

A brand often has a visual identity which appears as a logo, like the Nike swoosh or the Volkswagen VW roundel found on the front of the radiator grille; a brand generally has a name too. The only example of a brand I can think of which had a logo and no name was the golden symbol use by his purpleness Prince Rogers Nelson while he was referred to in words as "The artist formerly known as Prince." Radley bags have a name and a tag in the shape of a Scottie dog. Vivienne Westwood uses an orb. The logo is a symbol, that shortcut for a brand which makes it easier to recognize the source of the product which carries it. When you see it, you use your past experience of that brand to make decisions about the product that is displaying it.

However, a brand and a logo are not the same thing. The logo is just a device which packs the brand identity into one instantly recognizable symbol.

Hands up everyone who would like more time for themselves. Everyone is too busy. The Internet was supposed to save us time, but all it has done is made it easier to do loads more work. We look around us for ways to shorten the time it takes to do essential tasks, things that make it easier to get on with our lives without having to pause to make another decision.

Incidentally, it is the emotional part of the brain that makes the decisions; the logical parts stack up the facts for and against, but the frontal lobe and the cerebral cortex, the most recently evolved bits, are where the activity takes place when we choose one option over another. We know this from studying people who have had damage to their frontal lobe or cerebral cortex, from external injuries or tumors which squash up and inhibit the work of the modern brain. We make decisions all the time: which words to use, which clothes to wear (some take longer than others), which route to take, what to pick first from a big pile of tasks. These decisions are based on emotions, although we are not necessarily conscious of it at the time.

Those of us who have (relatively) normally functioning brains make millions of decisions daily; each of these micro-decisions involves an almost instantaneous engagement of the emotional part of the brain. On the supermarket run we can buy things almost without thinking, speeding up our decisions by using information we already possess, hardly slowing our shopping trolleys as we circuit our familiar routes. Spotting a logo will trigger associations for us, links with our past experiences of the brand. They push our emotional buttons too. If we are familiar with a logo this helps us to make an instant decision and saves us precious time.

So as we are walking around a supermarket looking for apple juice and we see a range of brands, we will probably recognize the packaging, the names, and the logos of some of those on offer and think so quickly that it is almost unconscious:

"That's the one that tastes great but is quite expensive."

"That's the organic one which I would like to buy but it costs more than all the rest."

"That one is cheaper but I know it's made from concentrate."

"That one is cheapest of all, but it is made with added artificial preservatives."

We will weigh up the advantages and disadvantages in a very short time and choose accordingly. Probably, when we shop at the same supermarket every week, we don't even stop to think at all; we just grab the one we normally take, recognizing the shape, color, and name of the box or bottle. We give it a moment's thought only if there's a completely new one or if we work in the apple juice industry.

There are around 40,000 products in the average hypermarket. If we were to stop at every product, read the label, assess it against the other four available products to decide which one is best, we would be there for a fortnight. The short cuts and shorthand of brands and their logos make our busy lives simpler. We know where we are with familiar brands, which is why it is important for brand guardians to keep their standards consistent.

When I see a paperback with a small penguin on it in an orange background, I know it's a Penguin book. I cannot guarantee that I will enjoy reading it, but I do know that it will be well written and edited, very unlikely to have typographical errors in it, and that the pages will not fall out. I have bought three travel books recently whose pages have fallen out before I've even left the house, let alone made it to the airport. That particular brand is unlikely to feature on my shopping list in future. For me, its logo is now associated with interesting contents but bad glue.

Recently I bought a beautiful, striped sweater in Paris. When I put it on I noticed this logo-style metal thing sewn at hip level. I was traveling scissorless so I had to gnaw through the stitching with my teeth to get the damned thing off. However, that would seem to be going against the current trend; many people buy products precisely because it has the manufacturer's name or logo on it. Logos on clothing say "Look at me; I cost this much!" and that is exactly why a lot of people buy them, even if observers interpret that signal differently from the way it was intended.

When did you ever see a counterfeit product that didn't have a logo on it? They are bought by their billions precisely because people want those faked logos to say things about them which aren't quite true, but they wish they were.

11
Minimizing risk

When I was a small child, spending most of my one shilling pocket money on chocolate, there were new bars out all the time. I mourn the short life of the Rowntree's Mint Cracknel to this day – three squares of crackly, minty green sugar strands with a coating of milk chocolate. I think it was the three pieces that did it for me; you could get twos, but no one else did a three.

It wasn't just new products, there were whole new brand names to be discovered. Old Jamaica rum and raisin chocolate was recently brought back by Cadbury as a special edition to satisfy the calorific and emotional needs of reminiscing adults.

Nowadays it's not so popular to bring out a completely new brand; it's considered safer to launch a brand extension. As I was saying earlier, the fashion houses tend to go into fragrance, accessories and make-up.

So recently we have had a limited edition orange KitKat from Nestlé (pronounced 'nessells' when I was a kid until it decided to show its multinational roots and insist on the proper Swiss–French pronunciation) and even green tea and sesame seed versions in Japan. Yesterday I bought a packet of Aero Bubbles, a sub-brand of Mint Aero which in the 1960s or 1970s would have been brought out with a completely new name. Mars have launched the Mars Delight, rather than just "Delight." (There are probably some trademark things going on with Cadbury's Turkish Delight that I don't know about, but you get the point.) Mars are giving the Delight a branding piggyback ride by making sure that customers know it's one of theirs; there is less of a buying decision to be made if people think it's a new version of a Mars bar they already know and like.

The reason for this is that all marketers are taught a theory by a chap called Igor Ansoff. He developed a matrix in 1965 (a little one, only two by two) which postulated that staying in your own area of expertise is your safest bet, given that you don't get complacent and assume that someone else won't come in and do it better. To grow your business all you have to do is sell more of the same to a similar bunch of people (market penetration, he calls it).

After that, if you want your business to grow further you can either find a new market – start selling your products to a whole new bunch of people (market extension) – or sell your current customers a different type of product or service (product development).

The biggest risk is to "diversify:" to bring out a completely new product and sell it to an entirely different market.

Marketers who are trained in the theory of their trade are encouraged to minimize risk, to avoid losing their employers' money, so the Ansoff matrix is trotted out on a regular basis to justify their decisions, no doubt popping up daily in PowerPoint presentations around the globe.

Launching an entirely new brand is seen as product development, but launching a new product *with the same brand name* is only market penetration, generally seen as around four times less risky! So you bring out a new product to add to your range and your brand becomes even better known and more recognizable. In the 1960s and 1970s, before marketers had learned this, new products popped up like mushrooms round a tree stump. Call me a saddo but I think the chocolate market was more fun back then before Ansoff's theory restricted the rampant creativity.

That's why when Mars brought out Mars Milk in black, red, and yellow packaging, they didn't call it Venus, put it in a green carton, and have to start all over again spending advertising money to launch something entirely new. When they bought out ice creams, they gave us Mars, Milky Way, Bounty, Twix, Snickers, and Topic ice creams and absolutely delicious pieces of frozen confectionery they are too. It's certainly pretty easy to feel safe and secure about what you're going to get when you buy one for the first time.

There is a cautionary tale and interesting diversion which concerns the first launch of Mars ice creams. It was entirely scuppered when Mars realized that all the fridges in confectionery shops in the United Kingdom were owned by their rivals, Walls. Were Walls going to allow Mars to share space with their own established brands, in fridges provided for the retailers for the sales of their own ice creams? Oh no, they were not. This is why in the United Kingdom you will find two fridges, one for Walls ice cream and one for Mars ice cream, in your corner shop. If you spend all your time on your marketing and forget about your distribution, whatever your brand is called, you can find yourself in a high-risk businesses.

You can see the marketers' point. Many of the biggest brands have been around for a hundred years. According to Rita Clifton, chair of Interbrand, 50 percent of today's brands have been around for 50 years. However, times change and not all of them can rely on their history to carry them onwards. Look at Google, Starbucks, Red Bull, and Apple or some of my favorite new things: Muji, Green & Black's, innocent, Lush, and eBay. Minimizing risk is not always the best strategy, but copying your own success is perfectly legitimate, if a little unimaginative; the next step amongst the morally challenged is to copy someone else's.

What if you were an entrepreneur who is not particularly bothered by ethical considerations? To take almost all of the risk out of launching a new business, what better way than to counterfeit someone else's desirable products? If the profits are high enough to offset the risk of seizure and confiscation of your goods, and you can set up a good enough cash paying network to avoid being caught as the operation's top dog, then why not? Someone else has done all the work. Thanks, Mr. Ansoff, we're off to make our fortune.

12
People do weird things while abroad

The *Observer* newspaper travel section carried Kathryn Flett's review of her trip to the Greek Island of Mykonos. She described being a little intimidated by the yacht dwellers who came to shore dressed to the nines in their luxury clothes and designer sunglasses to see and be seen at Psarou beach. Later in the trip at a less exclusive venue, she bought a pair of counterfeit Dior sunglasses for €15. She called them a "knock-off" which never sounds quite as illegal as counterfeit. At the end of her break she revisited Psarou, "fully tooled-up with my snide Dior glasses, real Dior sandals and freshly painted toes" as she put it.[22] Here you have an author and journalist, buying a pair of counterfeit sunglasses, but making sure we know that she owns genuine Dior sandals. Would she buy fake sunglasses in the United Kingdom? I would forecast otherwise.

What else happens on holiday? Here are people's stories from our research:

> My mom bought me a fake Burberry purse from Spain but she didn't know what it was. Mom said she got it from a street market at a cheap price.

> On holiday in Turkey I never bought anything, but the fakes were rife there; some of my friends bought fake Tommy Hilfiger tops and fake Louis Vuitton bags.

> I bought a Louis Vuitton handbag (not for me) from a back-street retailer in Dubai, not openly on sale, never mentioned if it was real or not. The whole secret thing was a hoot. Waste of time really, as my wife never appreciated the effort I went to.

> I bought a fake Gucci watch on a Spanish beach! Man came up to me on a beach with a briefcase of

Gucci watches, I was with my mum and we bartered as we were buying a watch each. They cost about £10 each (this was about six years ago). They were fun and I was on holiday.

Street Vendor in Cape Town. Price was real cheap (25 percent of real price), brands were openly on sale, and yes, the vendor was convinced they were the genuine article. I was a student at the time – ha, I still am a student! I was a young student at the time!

My uncle asked me to buy him a fake watch from the street vendors. He swore they lasted longer than the real things. And on the off chance it didn't, he could buy another one and not fret over any potential damage or wear (to the watch and his pocket).

I have bought a fake pair of brand name jeans over-seas. I have been given fake handbags (Gucci, Prada) and I use them (on impulse) cos' they are new and fashionable looking. I don't [generally] buy fake clothing/accessories since I am conscious of the fact that it is a fake and of lesser quality. I bought a pair of fake Prada jeans in Taipei, Taiwan. It was at a jeans shop. It was at least seven or eight years ago. I did not negotiate since I knew it was a fake and the price should definitely be more reasonable than the real thing. The brands were all openly on sale. The seller claims that it is the real thing, but I would doubt it cos' of the price I paid. It was an impulsive purchase – the seller was announcing on a loud speaker the sale of these brand name jeans while I was waiting for a cab.

Once I bought a fake Calvin Klein belt on holiday in Tenerife in about 1994, the seller said it was real but I knew it wasn't, but it was leather which was what I wanted. Negotiated the price on street where they were all laid out for sale. Functional, cheap and looked OK.

I bought some fake Oakley sunglasses in Vietnam this summer. I had to buy some sunnies as I'd lost mine. They were clearly fakes – although the seller tried to pass them off as the real thing. I paid about $2 or $3 (US) for them. He originally tried for about $20. My fake Oakley sunglasses lasted about a week before crumbling into many small pieces. Fake goods are generally poor quality and don't last as long. They start to come apart easily.

I got an LV Key Purse in Malaysia eight years ago ...still using it! It is from a flea night market in Kuala Lumpur and the price was 15 ringit ... less than £3. The seller did not convince me they were real when they look obviously fake! [Bought] just because it looked quite nice and I needed a key purse then so it was a bargain.

People who would never dream of breaking the law at home seemed to forget that other countries' laws also count as illegal. Buying fakes in Hong Kong was one of the touristy things everyone does like going bungee jumping in New Zealand, taking a helicopter trip around New York, or having your portrait sketched in Paris with the Sacré Coeur in the background.

One of the reasons that counterfeit copies of luxury brands developed their appeal was that 20 or 30 years ago you had to go somewhere exotic to get them. A fake Gucci watch was the kind of thing that your rich relatives wore to complement their tans when they got back from Thailand. They would never try to convince you it was real; they would show you that there was only plastic where the sapphire should be, then demonstrate the mythological difference between a real and their fake Cartier by showing that you could see the second hand moving tick by tick. Real luxury brands weren't really for people like us; they were for the seriously wealthy. The fakes were a little more accessible. It wasn't even the item itself which was interesting; it was the story of how it came to be purchased: the invitation to follow someone into a back street, through a courtyard, up some stairs and into a little office where the counterfeits would be unwrapped. Your friend would tell a tale about the worry about being stopped by customs on the way back through the airport, of adrenaline making her heart bump, suddenly terrified about being caught and questioned, thinking how silly she had been getting excited about a $10 watch, and promising herself she would never fall for it again.

At that time there was nowhere near as much overseas business or holiday travel. A fake Hermès scarf from Hong Kong's Stanley Market was a symbol of the exotic: something tempting, daring, and forbidden. Fakes were exclusive in their own way. They were cheap but not everyone could have them. With a real Cartier watch, all it takes to get one is money; a fake took ingenuity and access to opportunities which not everyone had. They took trouble, time, and dedication to obtain. They had to be stalked, hunted down, bargained for, and smuggled home. Getting one was a triumph. Fakes had a brand identity of their own. For some, they had a certain cachet which came with being illegal, although many found the concept of counterfeits tawdry and repellent, particularly if they had been brought up with a traditional set of moral values.

The UK Customs and Excise website list Counterfeit and

Pirated Goods as "Prohibited Goods (Goods which are banned completely)" from import into the UK:

> Counterfeit and Pirated goods, and goods that infringe patents when brought into the UK from outside the UK (such as watches, clocks and CDs, and any goods with false marks of their origin).[23]

The French Government stated in 2001 on its US Embassy site:

> IPR violations (trade- or servicemarks, copyrights, patents, industrial designs, etc...) attract, under French general Criminal Law, a sentence of two years' imprisonment and a fine of one million francs. Those penalties are doubled in the case of a repeated offense or where the violator is or has been related to the injured IPR holder.
>
> As far as imports or exports of counterfeit trademark goods are concerned, they are also offenses under Customs Law and attract the following additional sentences:
> - up to three years' imprisonment;
> - forfeiture of the counterfeit goods, as well as of the involved conveyances (vehicle, vessel or aircraft);[25]
> - a fine at least equal to the value of the goods, but not exceeding twice that value.[24]

Ghana prohibits the import of "Goods bearing fraudulent trademarks or infringing any copy-right."[26] Currently Indonesia only prohibits the import of counterfeit money.[27] New Zealand prohibits many fascinating things including dog semen and rubber hot water bottles but also "Goods bearing a label etc. which contains a false or misleading representation, such as to their country of origin, quality and so on." [28]

US Government Customs website gives statistics on the volume of counterfeit goods seized, however when downloaded from their website, they are displayed on screen rotated 90 degrees to the left and they are fitted with some smartypants software which prevents their being printed. I would tell more, but looking at the statistics at a 90 degree angle is uncomfortable. You can see details at www.customs.gov.

In 2003 they made 6,500 seizures worth over $94 million of which:

- 44 percent was from cigarettes
- 14 percent from clothing
- 12 percent from handbags, wallets, and backpacks
- 8 percent from media (including electronic media such as DVDs)
- 4 percent consumer electronics
- 3 percent watches and parts
- 3 percent footwear
- 2 percent sunglasses
- 1 percent headwear
- 6 percent everything else.[29]

That's $1.9 million of counterfeit sunglasses seized, and you can bet that many more are getting through than are being caught.

Of 2003's confiscated counterfeit goods, 66 percent came from China and the second largest source was Hong Kong at 8 percent, although Hong Kong is no longer a manufacturing base; it imports from China. Canada and Switzerland feature at numbers eight and nine on the list, with 1 percent of the market each. In 2002 Taiwan featured second with 27 percent of $98 million worth of seized goods (China was first at 49 percent) but by 2003 it had completely disappeared from the list.

China is massive in the cigarette market; 75 percent /$36 million of the goods seized from China in 2002 were cigarettes (64 percent/$33 million in 2003), but between 2002 and 2003 Chinese-seized handbags, wallets, and backpacks increased by 560 percent, reflecting the ever increasing demand for them.

Customs departments concentrate on consignments of counterfeit goods, the container loads which arrive in merchant vessels holding tons of merchandise and land on docks with false identification and paperwork among thousands of other containers. They will also stop and charge individuals who are bringing quantities of counterfeits home from their trips abroad, but this does not locate the source of the problem. What they need is a link back to the manufacturers and the importers who are profiting from this huge, illegal trade.

If a company wants its trademarks, copyrights, or patents to be protected by Customs departments, it can file an application, complete with the proof that it owns the intellectual property concerned, then Customs will check imports against the files they hold and confiscate accordingly. The US Department of Homeland Security currently charges $190 per application fee for each class of goods.

The law threatens the same punishments for importing counterfeit handbags or cigarettes. However, the fake cigarettes are likely to kill people (rather faster than real ones do) so ethically you could argue that concentrating on cigarettes would be the more important option.

There is a commonly held view that importing one or two little fakes isn't "really" illegal; it is. However, if you look very hard on the US Government Customs site you will find the following:

> travelers arriving in the United States may be permitted an exemption and allowed to import one article of each type, which must accompany the person, bearing a counterfeit, confusingly similar

or restricted gray market trademark, provided that the article is for personal use and is not for sale.

This exemption may be granted not more than once every 30 days. The arriving passenger may retain one article of each type accompanying the person. For example, an arriving person who has three purses, whether each bears a different infringing trademark, or whether all three bear the same infringing trademark, is permitted only one purse. If the article imported under the personal exemption provision is sold within one year after the date of importation, the article or its value is subject to forfeiture.[30]

Travelers are guilty of artistic license when it comes to interpretation of this exemption from the law, relying on the hope that the government is not really concerned with little people like us, that it's the big boys they want to catch.

What signal does this send to intrepid US citizens who venture abroad? That it doesn't really matter just to buy one or two little things? So how can it make a difference if they choose to buy a new purse every 30 days from a street market back home? How about two? How about 20? On returning from Kuala Lumpur with the latest high-quality fake Christian Dior bag, our traveler should remember that if she sets foot in France or the United Kingdom, she breaks the law. It is the same bag, manufactured by the same Chinese factory, breaking the same international IP protocols, but the law and interpretation of the law varies.

Pragmatically speaking; if every single US tourist who brought home a counterfeit purse had to be charged and tried; the court system would be log jammed until the next millennium. The US government has made the practical decision to overlook the small stuff. Perhaps up there in the

Senate is a traditional American who thinks it wouldn't do those "Old Europe" brands any harm at all to get a little poke in the eye once every now and again. Rubber stamping a little regulation which legally permits a few hundred thousand counterfeits into the country every year, as long as they are purchased directly from the little guy doing the ripping off, while keeping hundreds of thousands of Americans happy, what's the harm?

Here's my own tale of a hunt for a counterfeit bag. I wanted to see how easy or difficult it was to find one. I was in New York on Memorial Day weekend with the rest of the tourists, plus the fleet. Outside Bloomingdale's in the late afternoon, men started to arrive with barrows loaded with bags, fairly blatant copies of the latest luxury branded goods, but without the actual logo styles. They also had piles of black bin-bags by the side of the barrows from which they would produce the genuine fakes. I had a look at a Louis Vuitton counterfeit bucket bag decorated with Murakami's smiling cherries. It looked like good quality to me. I checked it against the real thing across the street later and I was even more impressed at the effort the counterfeiters had gone to rip off the original; the stitching matched, the lining was identical, even the color along the side seam was convincing. The vendor offered it to me for $140. He would have bargained if I would have been bothered, but I couldn't.

eLuxury.com, the LVMH Internet store where you can legally buy new Louis Vuitton goods only, didn't have one but offers the monogram canvas version for $865. As Bloomingdale's closed for the evening their shoppers passed the Louis Vuitton official outlet just before spilling out through the art deco doors on to Lexington Avenue. The street traders were ready to mop up any spare cash from would be LV owners whose budgets didn't stretch to the real thing. I went back on the holiday Monday to sneak some photographs of them, but there was no sign of them at all. Perhaps they are making enough profit to work weekends only.

Next I headed downtown to Canal Street which I had heard was the place to pick up the bargain bogus brands. It was a warm sunny day which made the tackiness seem more palatable. Packs of teenagers were swarming along the sidewalks, showing each other the contents of their economy black plastic carrier bags, making statements which sounded like questions:

"I got a Kate Spade?"

"I got the Dior?"

"I got the LV with the cherries?"

The Von Dutch fake hats and t-shirts were on full display along with shops full of fragrances which looked to me exactly like the genuine article. The bags were all copies but not counterfeits, badly done, obviously not made from leather, and very dodgily printed. One small Chinese woman stood in a doorway, waving an equally small Louis Vuitton monogram canvas purse and chanting, "Louis, Louis."

Over the street I stopped to look at the fold-out displays of watches: "$10," said the vendor. "Last week they were $35!"

These all carried real brand names from Swatch to Cartier. I chose the one I thought was the just about the most vulgar, unwearable item I'd ever seen because if I bought one I wanted to make sure it was really for research and not out of any desire to wear the thing. It was marked Chopard and the strap said Happy Sport. It is a chunky, silver colored thing with a shiny blue face, a case decorated with hundreds of tiny fake diamonds and three small fishes studded with blue, yellow, and pink sparkly stones rattling around inside it. I was sure that the counterfeiters hadn't really copied a real watch but had just invented the silliest thing they could think of. Although it says "Chopard Genève Swiss Made" on the back it also has a sticker on the strap which says "Made in China." So far it has kept perfect time. I looked up Chopard's website when I got home and was fairly gobsmacked to find that they really do make such an item. When I discovered that the real thing retails at about $10,000 my rational brain started to melt and I did seriously wonder if I should start wearing it. Has something gone strangely wrong with the world when you can buy a counterfeit copy which costs one-thousandth of the price of the original?

I stuck my head into a small shop which opened fully on to the street and examined the copies. "Louis Vuitton? Gucci? Dior?" asked the assistant. "Yeah, OK," said I, and I was shown into a small back room lined floor to ceiling with genuine faux designer bags. I spotted a Louis Vuitton Alma with a Murakami cartoon on it. "$35," said the girl. I was astonished at how cheap it was; it was one of those afternoons. "And this one," I asked, pointing to a cherry blossom Murakami design. "$40," but it was getting a bit hot in the small back room by then, so she pointed at the first one and said, "You can have that one for $30." I took it. When we got to the till I was charged my additional 8 percent New York sales tax. It may have been illegal to buy my trademark-challenged bag, but the transaction was perfectly legitimate. The real thing (without the cartoon) currently costs $795. It was so easy and such a bargain that I could see why so many people do it.

If I knew nothing about counterfeiting and intellectual property theft I would think that for $30 it is an excellent bag. Knowing that the manufacturers, shippers, and vendors run the risk of having all their stock seized, I'd have thought $30 is far too little to charge for it. Perhaps the US Government has decided to stop raiding Canal Street and instead settle for its regular 8 percent tax. Does that mean that the state of New York is living off immoral earnings?

13
Is this the real thing?

Lush boss Mark Constantine recently told his creative team that he cannot tolerate fake fur. He has been campaigning against testing cosmetics on animals for decades, and enforces a strict police against buying from suppliers who test or fund animal testing on ingredients. He loathes real fur, but fake fur?

> Because it's got so good I can't tell the difference any more," he said. "I don't know who to hate.[31]

From our research:

> I should say I'm starting to resent the increasing deceptiveness of improved quality fakes. I avoid buying authentic styles that I otherwise adore because they have been exploited to nausea-inspiring degrees in the streets of NY. What's the point of a designer's creating unique designs using original lines if everybody's wearing it and cheapening the concept with low-quality interpretations?

One of the ultimate ironies in this tale of copies and counterfeits is that Louis Vuitton first started to make his luggage with the LV initials woven into the fabric to stop people copying his products! Now that counterfeiting is rife, and the LV symbol is recognized worldwide, it makes Louis Vuitton one of the most obvious targets.

There are some shameless handbag counterfeits which are produced appallingly; the print is out of register so the logos are blurred, the rivets lose their plating, the straps are imitation leather, the stitching comes loose, and the fabric develops wrinkles. I own a dreadful Louis Vuitton rip-off mobile phone case and cover, a bad copy of the Murakami cherry tree design in pink. Not only do Louis Vuitton not make mobile phone covers, but also they do not sell them from a cheap shop at the edge of London's Covent Garden Piazza for £4.95. Everything about it makes it perfectly obvious that it is a fake; only the seller's nonchalance in the face of an illegal transaction made it seem vaguely legitimate. I would have expected him to keep the brazenly illegal fakes under the counter and bring them out like smuggled diamonds, only if someone asked him. Instead they were up on the wall with the "Chanel," "Dior," "Gucci," and the inevitable "Burberry" fakes.

Antiques experts turn pots upside down to check their origins. They probably recognize the style, but they have a look at the mark to check whether it is an original or a copy. One of my childhood friends, Mark, is now an antique dealer; one freezing cold Saturday at Tynemouth market he showed me a small ceramic vase with Christopher Dresser's signature on the back.

"Heard of him?" he asked. It happened that I had, because Christopher Dresser had designed for Linthorpe Pottery in Middlesbrough in the late nineteenth century and as my family is from there, my mum has one of his pieces, picked up at a jumble sale for a few shillings decades ago. Now there has been an exhibition of his work at the V&A he is somewhat better known.

"Fake," said Mark. "If it was real it would have his mark stamped into the pot; this one has been painted on afterwards."

I have a lovely antique chaise longue, which is probably an Edwardian one, only 100 years old, a copy of Georgian one 100 years older than that. India is a large source of fake antiques, copies of furniture, and children's toys that are made to look ancient. They have made their way into British antique shops and pop up every now and again on television programs, exposed by experts who disappoint the hopeful owners by pointing out that they can buy 1000 similar items anywhere in the same town. Antique shops are places where the origins of the goods on sale can be wide and varied. Many dealers buy at auction, and anyone is free to take their belongings to an auction house and put them up for sale. In this way an antique dealer may have no idea where the original goods came from, but relies on the description by the vendor and the expertise of the auctioneer. Most reputable auction houses would spot such fakes, but not all of them.

Online auctions are practically free from scrutiny; they rely on the vigilance of their users to point out counterfeits – but as long as there are people who want to buy cheaply and people who want to sell counterfeits, there is a complicity of "I won't tell if you won't" which goes on between buyer and seller. Unfortunately there are also a lot of plain straight lies told in online auction descriptions, which are used to disguise some excellent counterfeits available as the real deal.

Here's a story from Marietta:

> I once tried to buy a Louis Vuitton bag on eBay, assuming it was real. The seller told me her boyfriend bought it for her, and she was selling it because she needed the money. I figured that was a believable enough story. When I received it, it was a VERY good fake, but I still quickly saw the difference, mostly in quality. Even the quality of the dustbag's fabric wasn't quite as good. I took it to Louis Vuitton to double check it, and it took them five minutes to officially declare that it was definitely a fake. At first glance, they couldn't tell. They had to view the interior of the bag to declare it a fake.
>
> I got my money back ($500) from the woman, who was based in CA, by tracking down her phone number and giving her a good dose of psychotic New Yorker attitude. I harassed her via telephone, scaring her half to death in the process. Despite her

use of multiple names and addresses, I had solved the puzzle of where she really lived, and I threatened to hop onto a plane and show up at her door to get my refund. 'Cuz at that point, it wasn't even a matter of money; it was a matter of principle and I made sure she knew that.

But then she tried to resell it (or to sell another one just like it) to someone else, and the buyer contacted me to help her get her money back. By the end of it, the seller altogether left eBay.

I'm far more cautious about buying goods on eBay now. I demand photos of the authenticity cards, receipts, etc. before buying any name brand items on there now. (And I'm pretty much an expert at spotting fakes and knowing exactly where authenticity tags should be placed inside the bags, etc. This is because I know the brands so well now. So there's really no getting over on me.)

If you want to know if yours is real, then take it to a legitimate retailer. Better still, if you really want a genuine Louis Vuitton, buy from one of their shops, or from a legitimate second-hand dealer in Tokyo.

Here's a tale I was told about a woman who took her haul from a Chinese shopping trip into a Louis Vuitton shop to ask if it was real or not. This is entirely unsubstantiated, but the story goes that LV exchanged her very good fakes for their own products provided that she gave them the name of her contact and the exact location of the place she had bought them. I wouldn't bother trying the same thing; the brand owners are now well aware of the problem and have used intellectual property law to fight the issue without stemming the flow of goods into the market.

With the millions of items for sale at any one time on eBay, given that it is a database driven system which depends on the honesty of its buyers and sellers (and their feedback system), if there are people using it who want to buy counterfeits, then there will be sellers who will pop up with them to offer. I had a look at some bags advertised on eBay as LV Murakami limited editions. It is not difficult to find out about more these bags, if you are so inclined. The story is well documented. Louis Vuitton had a huge market in Japan, 75 percent of their sales at one point, but when other designers ventured East with more interesting looks, Vuitton lost sales as their brown and beige bags started to look rather staid in comparison.

When Bernard Arnault took over LVMH he brought in designer Marc Jacobs who invited Japanese artist Takashi Murakami to create a completely new look. Murakami created his "Eye Love" monogram designs which used 33 different colors and were notoriously difficult to screen print. Japanese women queued around the block and the bags sold out on the first day of their launch, then were soon changing hands at up to $7500. Their design is *kawai* style: that uniquely Japanese, large-eyed cartoon concept; the word means something along the lines of cute, loveable, sweet, and adorable. A London art gallery was recently selling a genuine signed limited edition of the Murakami Eye Love artwork; only 50 were produced.

14
An Internet adventure

So, I would consider it unlikely that the backpack I found on eBay at a starting price of £20 is the genuine article. Here's the description:

> ladies Louis Vuitton backpack bought last summer. I have used it a few times but it is still in excellent condition, it came with the care card, LV dust bag, gift envelope [not used]. It would be ideal for carrying all baby stuff around, or as a really posh schoolbag.!!

(You will observe that it even has handy product usage suggestions!)

While I was looking on the web for something to prove whether or not Louis Vuitton ever manufactured a bag in this style, the first listing on Google, before Louis Vuitton's own site came up, was this:

> OUR SPECIALITY IS 7 STAR TRUE MIRROR IMAGE REPLICAS IN LOUIS VUITTON AND CHANEL WHOLESALE AND RETAILS
>
> 10 PIECES (MIX ALLOWED)
>
> WE ARE THE LEADERS IN TOP QUALITY DESIGNER INSPIRED REPLICAS.
>
> WE WILL DROP SHIP HANDBAGS FOR YOU AND PROVIDE UPDATED TRACKING NUMBERS FOR YOUR CUSTOMERS.
>
> START EARNING HUGE PROFITS ON EBAY SELLING REPLICAS DESIGNER INSPIRED HANDBAGS
>
> MAKE MASSIVE EXTRA INCOME.
>
> WE WILL WHOLESALE TO YOU AND TEACH YOU JUST HOW TO HAVE THE SUCCESSFUL HOME PARTY FOR HANDBAGS. WE HAVE THE LATEST STYLES AND DESIGNS

WE WILL BE THE KEY TO YOUR SUCCESS GO WITH THE PROVEN LEADER

WE OFFER FREE SHIPPING WORLDWIDE !! FOR ALL OUR ITEMS

WE GUARANTEE 100% DELIVERY THROUGH CUSTOMS DELIVERED WITHIN 4–7 DAYS Our LV'S 7 STAR MIRROR IMAGE BAGS ARE MADE WITH: AND COME WITH: OXIDIZING LEATHER 100% genuine leather and oxidised cowhide leather YKK ZIPPERS MADE FROM SAME MATERIALS AS ORIGI-NALS UPSIDE DOWN LV'S ON DESIGNS THAT APPLY BRASS HARDWARE RASPBERRY ALACANTRA LINING CORRECT MARKINGS AND SIZES MODEL AND SERIAL NUMBERS

33 COLOR MURAKAMIS

DUST BAG, LV CARDS, CARE BOOKLET, COPY OF A RECEIPT OF A LV'S STORE OUR WHOLESALE PRICES

MONOGRAM CABAS PIANO $79 MONO-GRAM COMPACT WALLET $29 MONOGRAM COSMETIC POUCH $29 MONOGRAM DEAUVILLE $85 MONOGRAM MINI SAC HL $59 MONOGRAM PAPILLON $79 MONO-GRAM POUCHETTE ACCESSORIES $49 MONOGRAM PORTE TRESOR INTERNA-TIONAL$29 MONOGRAM SPEEDY 30 $69 ...MADE WITH THE BEST LAMBSKIN LEATHER JUST LIKE THE ORIGINALS

THE CHANEL BAGS WILL ALL COME WITH THE AUTHENTICITY CARD (WITH HOLOGRAM SERIAL NUMBER THAT IS THE SAME AS THE INTERIOR SERIAL NUMBER), DUST BAG, AND CARE BOOKLET. CHANEL CAMBON LINE SMALL WHITE TOTE $79

CHANEL CAMBON LINE BLACK MULTI-POCKETS BAG $99 etc..

Technically, I am breaching their copyright by using more than 200 words without applying for permission, but my own ethics do not extend to respecting the intellectual property rights of counterfeiters. They not only copy the bags to the best of their ability, they are now offering faked till receipts from bona fide Louis Vuitton stockists. To rub salt into the wounds they even have better techniques for getting their websites placed higher in the search engines' results tables than the real brand! (I rarely use exclamation marks but I feel that this one is justified.)

(The above text will probably divide readers into groups: those who are astonished and appalled at this blatant, illegal trade in counterfeits, those who can't understand what the fuss is about handbags, and those who are slightly annoyed that I didn't put the web address in a note.)

In fact, of the first ten websites (of 185,000) which pop up on a Google search for "Louis Vuitton Eye Love," eight are for counterfeit bags, one is for the genuine screen printed limited edition artwork, and one is for a bag selling on eBay which has already reached $7,350 with two days to go. If people are prepared to pay that for the real second-hand one, then perhaps it is unsurprising to find that fakes flourish. The counterfeiters in the first eight sites euphemistically call them faux, mirror image, replica, and even fake, but none of the wholesalers claim that they are the real thing; they leave that to the sellers.

I also found a conversation which took place between November 2004 and February 2005 amongst on a forum called Teen Today;[32] five contributors involved and it went like this [unedited]:

Subject: louis vuitton speedy bag

1) I want one for christmas but i dont wanna spend over £50 i have looked on eBay and they go up to about £150 has anyone got any ideas where i can get one from plus i dont wanna a fake one

2) whats a louis vuitton speedy bag?

3) do u want it in multicolour or monogram, i fink the monogram would be better.

am gettin either a dior bag or gucci for christmas 🙂 lol

4) im getting the multicolour ive gpot a dior bag

3) that would be the same as jessica simpson's wudnt it, awh ded cute!

4) yeah thats theone i want 🙁 🙁 i brought one on eBayer for £50and the bloke still hasnt snet it this was about 2 weeks ago 🙁

[three months later]

4) Its happened to me again 🙁 just brought another one of eBay for £60 and the owmen has been suspended so i might not get it.I think its just fate that i shouldnt get one of these bags

5) I don't think theres much hope of getting one under £50 the cheapest louis vuitton I have was £200 in a sale, I think your best bet is to keep trying on eBay !

4) they have got them on eBay i just got one for £60

5) omg !! wow okay then im getting myself on there now !!

[20 minutes later]

5) omg i just bidded a tenner on a real louis vuitton bag !! lol think im going to faint !!

Incidentally, at the time of writing, the cheapest Speedy bag available is $540 from the LVMH-owned eLuxury website. The one that our chatroom teen wants to buy costs $1670. There is no shadow of a doubt that every "Vuitton" bag referred to in the above chat is a counterfeit. Also, Louis Vuitton never discount their bags so the one which number five says she saw for £200 in a sale was also a counterfeit. These girls (especially number 5) are happy to convince themselves that their longed-for bags stand some chance of being genuine bargains.

While I was on the Teen Today website the following email arrived:

Subject: Replica Louis Vuitton Purses
- Looking to spoil your girlfriend/fiance/wife?
- Got yourself into trouble and looking for a way out?
- Just looking to get a little more action?
- Does she just want a nice bag but can't afford the real one?

Get her a replica Louis Vuitton Handbag!

These purses sell in stores from $500 up to over $2,500!!! our prices range from $50–$220. It is nearly impossible to tell the difference between these and the real ones.

Finally, I arrived at the Louis Vuitton site and found that the design pictured on eBay was never made by Louis Vuitton.

The counterfeiters have copied the monogrammed print but made up a backpack style which you can buy in Japan in the standard Monogram style, but not in the Eye Love multi-color. However, arriving at that point was an interesting journey.

What happened next:

The fake Eye Love backpack's highest bid price stayed at £42 for two days but I kept checking to see how it was getting on.

2 mins 37 seconds to go and the price is up to £53.00.

2 mins 11 secs ... I wonder how much people are prepared to pay for   these things.

1 min 48 secs ... I could try it and find out!

1 min 33 secs ... Should I bid for an illegal counterfeit bag?

1 min 14 secs ... What I am thinking?

28 secs ... I enter my maximum bid £100; surely someone will pay more than that?

23 secs ... I am the maximum bidder at £54.20.

13 secs ... I am still the maximum bidder at £65.00.

9 secs ... My rival bids £68.00 so I am forced up to £69.00.

5 secs ... £72.00.

2 secs ... £78.00.

... Oh bother! I have bought a fake bag for £78.00

I shall have to hang it on the wall like a hunting trophy or a piece of Takashi Murakami's art. Obviously I can't use it. Anyone I know who knows anything about posh bags would know it was a fake and everyone I know who wouldn't spot it as a fake would either think I was stupid for spending that much on a bag or would be impressed for the wrong reasons. Paradoxically, I reckon that the only people who would think it was just a really nice leather bag with an interesting pattern on it would be those who have never heard of Louis Vuitton, like my mum and Auntie Viv. Besides, this is not about what other people think of it, it's about what I think of myself for buying a fake; the more I think about it the more it makes me feel ill that I bid for it.

Maybe I can justify it as research.

The next day I got this in my email:

> Dear Sarah McCartney,
> The following listing:
> 6758746306 - Louis Vuitton Backpack ... Murakami Multicocre eYE.
> has been removed from eBay for violating eBay policy. Since this listing was removed, you are not required to complete the transaction.
> For a complete list of eBay's policies, please visit:
> http://pages.eBay.co.uk/help/sell/item_allowed.html
> Regards,
> Customer Support (Trust and Safety Department)
> eBay Inc

Saved! Despite all the millions of transactions taking place on eBay, they are keeping a close eye (no irony intended) on the counterfeit market after all. Perhaps someone from LVMH is employed to spot fakes of all their brands, which include Fendi, Loewe, Celine, Pucci, Christian Dior, Marc Jacobs, TAG Heuer, Donna Karan, Kenzo, Krug, Givenchy, Guerlain, Benefit, Aqua di Parma, Fred, Chaumet, Fresh, Thomas Pink, Moët et Chandon, and Hennessey, plus the shops to sell them in: Sephora, sephora.com, eLuxury.com, Samaritaine, and Le Bon Marché.

In 2003 and 2004 LVMH made a gross profit of over 60 percent and in 2004 their operating profit was 19.2 percent. This is phenomenal. Somehow it is difficult to feel sympathy for them when their designs are copied and they complain that this is eroding their profits. I do think it is unacceptable to copy their designs – it is lazy, immoral, and stifles creativity – but if there is a 60 percent margin in there, it is not impossible to understand why the criminal or just the amoral opportunist mind might be attracted to the business.

I admit, I would have liked to have inspected this bag to see how good or bad a fake it was. If it was as good as it looked on screen then it would have been a very good quality bag for £78, but it would never have left the house because, I admit it, I do care what the people I know would think about it.

I think what I shall do is spend the money on a bag made to my own design by someone who makes a living from leather work. Talking of which ...

15
Cabbage and the European trainer mountain

I have a bag made by a craftworker in Washington (County Durham, UK, not DC). It was designed to my mum's specifications and made from dark red patent leather with a flower print on it. His supply came from the tannery which supplies Doc Martens, the boot company. He buys a lot of their leftovers and makes them up into belts, handbags, coin-purses, and other small goods.

Purveyors of counterfeit goods often try to convince you that they'd done the same thing. In 1992 I was taken to a supermarket in Casablanca where the group of travel trade people I was with went bananas about all the bags for sale there. I'd never heard of Louis Vuitton at the time and wasn't particularly impressed by the brown and beige monogram thing – too muddy for me – but the women I was with were lugging as many of these fake "Keepall" and "Speedy" bags to the till as they could carry and clutching them like long-lost children. We were told they were "cabbage," the trade's name for fashion goods cut out of leftover material, and that they came from the factory that Louis Vuitton used in Morocco so they are "exactly the same, really."

I found two bags I liked the look of and paid £45 each for them; they were leather, silk lined, very smart, and had a Kenzo label on them. I'd never seen a real one and had no reason to question what I was being told. I suspected that I must be doing something wrong, in some vague way, but their explanations seemed reasonable and I didn't think that a retailer would have counterfeits on sale openly. Surely someone would catch him?

Back in the United Kingdom, a worldly chap who ran an advertising agency told me that what happens with "cabbage" is that manufacturers are given just enough fabric to make up the required order of say 500 bags. They are also given exactly the right numbers of branded rivets, zips, clasps, buckles, or whatever fitting are needed, made to a high standard. The manufacturer then skillfully cuts the

material so that there is some leftover, has the fittings repro-
duced, and runs up another few bags to sell for himself. I'm
sure that sometimes it happens like that. Probably in 1992
Moroccan factories were doing quite a trade in selling fake
designer goods to tourists.

Again, if you choose to do the research, you will find out
that Louis Vuitton have never manufactured in Morocco, only
in France and Spain where they can keep a close eye on quality control. The salespeople were making it all up, the ad
agency exec was mistaken, and the LV bags were 100 percent
counterfeit. Back in Morocco in 2004, I bought some leather
slippers in the Marrakech soukh; mine are pink, but if I'd
wanted I could have bought them made up in the classic LV
monogram, or in Gucci or Christian Dior's well-known
branded styles. You'd have to be seriously deluding yourself to
be convinced that these were genuine; to be fair, the vendors
were laughing as they swore on their lives that these were the
real thing. They will tell you what you want to hear. If you are
willing to be persuaded then there is always someone available
to sell you a genuine fake.

If you want to know if something you've bought is real, a
legitimate retailer will tell you. However, they absolutely will
not tell you how they know. They may disappear around the
back of the shop while they inspect it, then they return with
a definite answer. In the case of my lost eBay "Murakami"
bag it would be spotted in seconds; in fact I would probably
have to pick the assistants up off the floor and slap them
hard to stop them laughing. In Marietta's case it took them
several minutes. That is a long time to tell whether or not it's
one of your own genuine products.

You might expect them to come out and show how clever
they are to have spotted it by saying something like:

> Well, the reason we know is because that little
> detail just there, which you'd hardly notice if you

didn't know the design inside out, is the wrong
shade of red, and matched with the original you
can spot the slight difference...

They don't do this because you could have been sent in by
the counterfeiters for a bit of free consultancy on your quality control. Imagine. You'd be hot-footing it back to Shen-
zhen with a full report. A genuine retailer will tell you it is
real or they will tell you it is fake, but that is your limit.

In Paris once, Judy was approached by a Chinese woman
outside the Louis Vuitton flagship store. Judy is ethnic
Chinese too, but the woman had assumed she was Japanese,
probably because she was headed towards Louis Vuitton.
She took out a catalog and a wodge of euros, indicated the
exact style she wanted Judy to buy for her and offered her
$200 US to make the purchase. She said she wanted the bag
for her daughter but had already reached her permitted limit.
Vuitton shops in Europe are famously rumored to limit
Japanese tourists to three bags each although I reckon that
this rule has less to do with selling bags at lower European
prices and more to do with building the mythology of their
exclusivity. Judy declined the $200 but the next time she was
in Paris the woman was there again. She strongly suspects
that the mysterious buyer was acquiring bags to take home
and copy for the counterfeit trade.

There are rumors that if you do take the cash and buy a
bag then private security agents who are watching through
binoculars from the other side of the Champs Elysées will
swoop down and interrogate you, although I don't think you
can be arrested for selling a bag, even at a $200 profit.

All this serves to increase the glamorous, exclusive image;
these bags seem almost as precious as diamonds.

The last time we were in Paris, Judy and I amused ourselves
seeing if we could spot genuine and fake designer bags while
we drank coffee and watched the world go by. It's tricky if you

don't know exactly what details and designs you are looking for. We reckoned that the man in the brand new black cashmere coat, wearing Versace sunglasses and shiny black shoes, accompanied by his equally well-dressed family, was carrying a genuine Vuitton holdall. On the other hand, the woman with work-worn shoes and clothes was probably carrying a fake Burberry. If it's for sale on a market stall it's fake or possibly a gray import, just to leave you with a shadow of a doubt; if it's at Selfridges, Isetan, Le Bon Marché, KDV, Bloomingdale's, The Bay, or similar, then it's real.

We were baffled by a shop full of Adidas trainers off the Boulevard de Clichy, stacked high from the floor around the edges and in the middle. They looked real, right down to the boxes, but the set-up looked distinctly dodgy. They could have been legitimate: old stock which a wholesaler wanted to shift at low cost or bought from a bankrupt distributor. Perhaps they were stolen, or had been sold at low cost to Eastern Europe then brought back in as gray imports. Three out of four of us there were Adidas wearers and we couldn't see anything wrong with the shoes. All the same, we decided against, despite the low prices and that one of us present is a notorious bargain hunter. Perhaps the only way to tell is where you buy them, we reckoned we would stick with Foot Locker, Size?, and Oki-Ni in future.

The following day we were at the Musée de la Contrefaçon marveling at the counterfeits and copies, some very convincing and others very creatively assembled. On display was a pair of what looked like a special edition of Timberland boots, the ankle part made with Timberland's trademark tan leather and the toe in the Louis Vuitton monogram multicolore white leather with colored LV logos. No such shoe had ever been made by the genuine manufacturers. It is difficult to decide whether this is classed as stealing an idea or having a strange one of their own – however, they definitely stole Timberland's and Louis Vuitton's logos and so they were infringing intellectual property rights. They were using Timberland and Louis Vuitton's reputations for quality to sell boots which had no guarantees attached.

The temptation to make a saving is always strong, but we concluded that we had been right not to take the risk. All the same, we couldn't be certain; if they were fakes, they were good ones – at least to look at – but what if they didn't have the correct foot support for sport?

In 2004 I went to a very smart conference at the RAC Club, Pall Mall, all about excellence in business. Jimmy Choo was there in person. I had the opportunity to nod at him and he nodded back. (I treasure that.) There were speakers from Boden, Dyson, Tanner Kroll, and Tommy Hilfiger. Robert Bensoussan, chief executive and part owner Jimmy Choo (the company not the man) described how Mr. Choo himself was going to move into teaching to become shoe guru to a new generation of master craftspeople while he himself would expand the Jimmy Choo brand into previously uncharted territories, extending into the handbag market.

One person asked Fred Gehring, Chief Executive of Tommy Hilfiger Europe, after had made his presentation: "How do you feel when your clothing turns up in places like TKMaxx?" There was a lot of polite laughter around the room as the well-heeled audience generally believed that Fred would think this an appalling thing; certainly none of them would be seen in the likes of a discount shop buying the previous year's stock! I particularly remember the conversation as I was wearing a coat by Custo Barcelona, bought at TKMaxx for 40 percent of its usual price, which had been complemented several times by complete strangers I had met during the conference coffee break. I couldn't help but be amused by the audience's assumption that none of the delegates could ever stoop so low.

They were surprised by the answer.

Mr. Gehring, referring not by name to the difficult IP case that Tommy Hilfiger had fought against Tesco in the United Kingdom, said that he would much rather see his end of season goods being sold in TKMaxx, when he knew he could track the sales and guarantee that they were genuine, than find them ending up discounted in UK supermarkets when he had sold them to non-EU countries, only to find them back here as "gray imports."

In the UK, Tommy Hilfiger clothes were first widely publicized when Diana Princess of Wales was photographed with a huge logo over her back. Diana was credited with saving the UK hat and shoe industries, and her name could take a small brand and inflate it almost overnight to international success. When she wore flat shoes to avoid towering over Charles, Clarks Shoes who had been tottering along with not much hope of a future, suddenly picked up sales for their similarly shaped designs. In the United Kingdom and the United States the Tommy Hilfiger brand had been clothing for the sporty, sailing set; Hilfiger at the time reflected Diana's move out of public life into the social world of the leisured and wealthy, Monte Carlo yacht-owning classes.

Next, the music business embraced the country club set's look and hijacked the brand's identity. Seeing a new, larger market – there are more people who like listening to hip-hop than own their own yacht – the company had welcomed the increase in sales but the brand then began to suffer from its association with the US "gangsta" culture, particularly after a few high-profile drive-by shootings started to tarnish the bling.

It was time to grab back the brand, de-program it and reaffirm its original symbolic values. In the United Kingdom Tommy Hilfiger would not sell their clothing to the Tesco supermarket chain because the company felt that this was inconsistent with their reclaimed brand identity.

Tesco had had quite a few battles with brands when their owners had refused to supply them, including Sony, Nike, and Ralph Lauren. Tesco wanted to use the brands as stepladders to raise their own brand profile in the eyes of their customers. Tesco were hoping that they would attract more customers who would reconsider: "If Tesco are selling Ralph Lauren then they must be posher than I thought!" The brand guardians were concerned that their own customers would think: "If people can buy Ralph Lauren at Tesco then I'm donating all mine to charity."

Then what happened was that Hilfiger clothes turned up in Tesco stores; Hilfiger did a bit of sleuthing and failed to explain where the goods had come from, so they obtained a writ to stop Tesco selling "unofficially sourced" goods, having concluded that the goods must be counterfeits. In fact, Mr. Gehring explained, they had been exported at discounted wholesale prices by Tommy Hilfiger Europe to a non-EU country to reflect the price that this country's customers could afford to pay for them. They were finally able to track the links between their original customer and the eventual destination. Tesco had always maintained that they were the genuine article and proclaimed that they were crusading against restrictive practice: artificially inflated prices for designer goods.

What is interesting about this incident, from the observer's point of view, is that Tommy Hilfiger Europe themselves could not tell whether or not the clothing they bought from Tesco was counterfeit or not. If you want to be absolutely certain that your bargain is a legal, genuine bargain, go to TKMaxx or wait for the sales. But if the counterfeiters have got so good that even the brand names can't tell the difference between their own goods and the ripped off version, why would bargain-hunting customers pay a premium price for the real thing?

Here's a reason not to worry about your brand being devalued by being discounted:[33]

I always thought Antik Batik looked beautiful when I saw their clothes in magazines and editorials. I like to wear natural fabrics and having a dress made out of printed silk is a dream for me. I found a Antik Batik dress in TKMaxx, it was marked down from £185 to £25. I have never felt so beautiful as I do when I am wearing it, I have had strangers coming up to me in the street telling me how great I looked. I therefore felt it was worth the money to buy something from their new A/W 04/05 season at the "proper price". The dress was £160 but I felt I wouldn't find anything in silk in the stores like Top Shop, and that I would be unlikely to be lucky enough to find something again in TKMaxx. I noticed TKMaxx Antik Batik was changing hands on eBay for almost the full retail price. I therefore felt justified!

Let's wind up with a cautionary gray import story. In 1998 counterfeit designer clothes seized and confiscated in Yorkshire were sent as part of a humanitarian aid scheme to refugees in Eastern Europe. Shortly afterwards, a large shipment of the same clothes was seized once more from market stalls in Newcastle upon Tyne. Subsequent batches of designer fakes destined for refugee camps had their embroidered logos unpicked and their labels cut out, to avoid the likelihood of this happening again.

16
The earner–spender generation

Bagging a bargain has become an international sport. To find a fault-free cashmere sweater marked down by 75 percent is a triumph, the twenty-first century equivalent of using your foraging skills to bring home enough fruit and nuts to feed the family. Returning from the Kuala Lumpur night market with the absolute latest in Gucci copies isn't quite the same as using your skill with a spear to bag an antelope, but perhaps it gives us a similar feeling of triumph. We call it "bargain hunting" after all.

As the spending-not-saving culture has emerged in the West, particularly in the United Kingdom, our financial skills can paradoxically be demonstrated not by our ability to invest wisely, but by the savings we make on recommended retail price. Shopping skills deliver their benefits immediately. The purchaser is rewarded with instant satisfaction from carrying off a tangible article and the intangible "saving," but he or she can multiply that satisfaction by telling friends all about it!

For a shopper, acquiring a bargain is as gratifying as passing an examination but without the trouble of two years' preparation. Of course, the satisfaction is pretty short lived. But while many people are discovering that buying more things does not buy contentment, however much they desired them at the time, there are still millions who believe that it will, as long as they find the right things. There are others who are making a move towards less tangible but longer term achievements. Or perhaps that should be a move back, as these are aims which were widely accepted in the United Kingdom and United States before the free-range capitalism of Reagan and Thatcher altered our views.

Thirty or 40 years ago a worker entering employment aspired to the intangible aim of achieving "financial security." People made career decisions based on the pension schemes that their employers offered. Financial security is an odd thing which does not always depend on the amount of money you have saved up. If you have $1 million invested for your future and the value of it collapses to $500,000 you may feel dangerously unprotected against future financial events. If you had $10,000 in the bank and won $50,000 in the lottery, you would probably feel as steady as a rock.

In the United Kingdom the Pensions Commission estimates that up to 40 percent of the working population are not saving enough for their old age. We have started to live for today and claim our rewards on earth, right now, rather than saving for the future, including retirement. The Commission's first report[34] stated our options:

Either:
i) pensioners will become poorer relative to the rest of society or
ii) taxes/National Insurance contributions devoted to pensions must rise or
iii) savings must rise or
iv) average retirement ages must rise.

In other words, our widespread preoccupation with spending what we earn and our carefree attitude to stacking up our credit card debts must end or we will all have to work longer to be able to afford to retire. The report estimates that 9 million people are under-saving, "some by a small amount, some severely." The people whom it will affect most are those who plan to retire in 20 to 25 years' time. These are the ones who have not saved adequately and do not have much time to rectify their mistakes. The report speculates that some people may be relying on their potential inheritance money from their relatives' homes which have increased in value far more rapidly than the rise in wages over the last three decades. However, there's many a slip twixt cup and lip; house prices could collapse; inheritance tax in the United Kingdom is already affecting an increasing proportion of average people who find themselves living in valuable houses. Also, people are living longer, which means that the current generation of earner-spenders could be retired and surviving on an inadequate pension for decades while their doddering mums and dads are living it up into their nineties on household equity release schemes.

The United Kingdom and the United States, with the rest of Europe apparently catching up rapidly, has had a slow but widespread attitude shift away from financial responsibility over the past 30 years, and if what the press calls the pensions time bomb is going to be defused before it detonates, then we have to make a pretty rapid shift back again.

> The UK has the largest credit card market in Europe, with one credit card for every two adults. Spain comes second, with one in five adults carrying a credit card. In the UK, the total amount we put on our credit cards is three times more than the rest of Europe put together.[35]

In the early 1930s there were economic depressions in the Western World. America was particularly hard hit by poverty. From 1939 to 1945 when much of Europe suffered great hardships during wartime, and afterwards while economies struggled to recover, even basics like clothing and food were restricted. Many of our grandparents were brought up having learned to "make do and mend," scrimp and save. In the 1950s an exciting new affluence spread widely and touched all social groups.

Historian Eric Hobsbawm wrote of the post Second World War era:

> It was not that workers became unrecognisable as such, although strangely ... the new, independent youth culture from the late 1950s on took its

fashions in both clothes and music from the working-class young. It was rather that some sort of affluence was now within the reach of most, and the difference between the owner of a Volkswagen Beetle and the owner or a Mercedes was far less than that between the owner of any car and the owner of no car, especially if the more expensive cars were (in theory) available on monthly instalments. Workers, especially in the last years of youth before marriage and household expenses dominated the budget, could now be luxury spenders, and the industrialization of the couture and beauty business from the 1960s on immediately responded. Between the top end and the bottom end of the high-tech luxury markets that now developed – e.g. between the most expensive Hasselblad camera and the cheapest Olympus or Nikon that produced results while conferring status – there was only a difference of degree.[36]

Our tastes for luxury and our belief that we deserved it took hold.

17
When greed was good

Why should anyone not get what they want, and not get it now? Eastern philosophies encourage us to live in the present, but in the twenty-first century earner-spender society this is (deliberately or disingenuously) misinterpreted as living for the present. Living in the present is about learning from the past but accepting that it is over; there is little point in dwelling on its disappointments or harking back to its successes. Likewise, if we forget to appreciate the present but concentrate instead on how much better life will be in the future, then we shall find ourselves looking back and wishing we had enjoyed it more at the time.

Spending everything we earn and borrowing more so that we can have everything we want right now was not exactly what the Buddha meant.

As the traditional trappings of the privileged began to be shared in a more egalitarian manner – although the divisive invisible barriers themselves remained intact – we were encouraged, particularly in the 1980s, to believe that all we had to do was work hard, elbow our way to the top, trampling on the less ambitious on the way, and we could own everything we wanted.

We were also taught that owning things would make us happy, and this is still widely believed and promoted as a belief system, particularly in the United States. It is comforting to think that there might be an instant solution to our miserable moments and that all we have to do to lighten the gloom is buy something.

One of the greatest insults my grandmother, Elizabeth Bain (1898–1990), could throw at someone was, "He's got more money than sense, him!" It was in the 1980s that having more money than sense became something to be proud of. If you earned the money, you had the right to flash it around.

On Wall Street and in London's City institutions, financial speculations could earn huge profits and the resulting bonuses allowed loud young men to celebrate openly, keeping the vineyards of Champagne and the plantations of Colombia in business.

In 1987 the Hollywood film *Wall Street* told a tale of success based on greed and immorality ultimately being vanquished by integrity. In the spirit of the times, it was the shameless, power-hungry Wall Street corporate raider, Gordon Gecko, Michael Douglas's character, who was upheld as a shining example of how to make it in business. Audiences found fault with Gecko's character not because he was an evil, self-seeking, amoral stain on the face of humanity, but because he was outsmarted. Gordon's credo: "Greed is good!" combined with "Lunch is for wimps," became stock phrases for brash businesspeople to justify their selfishness in pursuit of profits and bonuses. Being horrid to achieve your aims became an acceptable way of working. King Ronald and Queen Margaret ruled over the Empire of Capitalism and where success was at stake, no holds were barred.

"Greed will not only save Teldar Papers, but that other malfunctioning corporation known as the United States!" said Gekko. The fallout is still raining on employees, investors, stakeholders, and unsuspecting customers as companies who used Gordon's words to justify their unsound working practices are imploding all over the world – but particularly in the United States.

Of course, one film doesn't change our entire culture; when Michael Douglas won the Oscar for playing Gecko it recognized and perhaps legitimized the Thatcher/Reagan teachings which were shunting society's accepted views sideways. Indeed, Thatcher told the British nation that there was no longer any such thing as society, which outraged many and encouraged others. It has been interpreted, reinterpreted, and argued over ever since; Google found me 47,300 references to the statement in 0.33 seconds. Here is what she said in full:

I think we've been through a period where too many people have been given to understand that if they have a problem, it's the government's job to cope with it. "I have a problem, I'll get a grant." "I'm homeless, the government must house me." They're casting their problem on society. And, you know, there is no such thing as society. There are individual men and women, and there are families. And no government can do anything except through people, and people must look to themselves first. It's our duty to look after ourselves and then, also to look after our neighbour. People have got the entitlements too much in mind, without the obligations. There's no such thing as entitlement, unless someone has first met an obligation.

In those times of high employment, Thatch's hand-knitted philosophy was interpreted by those who did not wish to accept responsibility for the temporarily or permanently less fortunate as, "Every man for himself: the devil take the hindmost." It accompanied Reagan's US and the UK governments' beliefs that every individual who worked hard could be a success and the only reason for unemployment was laziness. Mrs. Thatcher's style of Adam Smith economics produced a theoretically egalitarian, meritocratic approach, a change for the British Conservative party which, during most of the twentieth century, had traditionally backed the class system, the upper classes' rights to govern because they knew how to do it properly and the idea that the workers would be happiest if they knew their place.

The time was proclaimed as an entrepreneurial golden age as thousands of people set up small businesses with their redundancy payments from the "rationalization" of denationalized industries. In the United Kingdom there had in fact been more small businesses set up during the Labour government of Harold Wilson in the 1960s, but facts often give way to sound bites when the statistics are not readily available. According to Warwick Business School, who had done the research and found the facts, people were more likely to set up their own businesses in the 1960s when the fear of failure was not so great. Once the support system for the unemployed was dismantled, people were more likely to stay in their paid jobs than spring into self-employment, making it the norm for companies to expect longer working hours from those who considered themselves fortunate to have decent jobs.

When Chancellor Norman Lamont's Black Wednesday hit the city in 1992 and some of the hard-working, hard-playing City boys were turfed out of their lucrative numbers as their companies went out of business, it became pretty clear that it was not only hard work that kept you in a job. Sometimes, there were things beyond your control which kicked you out of your comfy chair. They had met their daily obligations, but there was no entitlement waiting for them after all. Cracks appeared in the façade and then in the foundations of the tough society-less society; talk of a new, kinder era began but took a while to catch on.

Drifting through the previous 100 years there had been a sense that governments intended life to get better for all. Everyone would have access to decent healthcare and education. The miner's son could rub shoulders with the landowner's daughter at university. Large corporations built sports centers for their staff and provided career training. The standard of living was generally expected to rise; all homes would be built with bathrooms, slums with no sanitation would be demolished. (Some of the developments built to replace them didn't go quite to plan, but the intentions were good.) Perhaps the affluent years of the 1950s and 1960s had encouraged people to expect state support in times of need, to believe that someone would always be there to take care of them.

A different kind of expectation flourished in the 1980s. The governments of Britain and the United States no longer saw it as their responsibility to promote equality of opportunity. You had to grab it for yourself. The ambitious 1980s youth developed an alternative view – that money could buy you status. Equality was no longer desirable; with whom exactly did you want to be equal? Everyone had been offered a glimpse of glamour; worlds that had seemed unattainable had lowered the ladder and all you had to do was buy your way up each step.

I remember the odd sight of a Rolls-Royce parked (squeezed) on to the drive of a 1930s semi-detached suburban house in Harrow. A man in our street had a Porsche. People would say, "Well, why shouldn't I? I earned it, it's mine to spend." As grandma would have said, "people were getting up themselves." Luxury brand extensions went into hyperdrive. Doormen at stores which previously served the "well-to-do" and well known, began to allow the vulgar but wealthy past their portals, although Harrods will still forbid people wearing shorts from venturing inside.

It had happened in previous centuries; industrialists had made their fortunes, bought their titles, and were absorbed into the ancient aristocracy by funding the restoration of crumbling stately homes. Henry James writes of American heiresses being courted by the titled sons of penniless European families, money mixed with titles and classes could theoretically change places. But this time it was a free-for-all. In the 1980s the trappings of wealth were worn on the outside for the first time. It was as if the grocer's daughter who married a millionaire had given everyone permission to show off their wealth.

The conditions had created a society in which the pursuit of money was the prime directive. In one small but influential population subgroup, whatever money could buy was important; if it couldn't be bought then it could therefore not have any significance. What made something worth having was how much it cost and once you owned it, your peers needed to know that it had cost you a fortune. Conversely, nothing that couldn't be bought could possibly be worth owning. Labels appeared on the outside of products; you carried your Burberrys' raincoat with the recognizable checked lining clearly showing. Yuppie culture had arrived.

18
Labeled with love

Young Urban Professionals (or young, upwardly-mobile professionals) aspired to the trappings of wealth but without being disturbed by its art forms (unless they were very expensive).

Yuppies aspired to the UK "Sloane," US "Preppie," or French BCBG style of living – but without the culture because that would have taken too long to assimilate. Books took too long to read, museums and galleries were free and therefore worthless, unless they were showing something you could buy at the end of it. I worked for a man who adopted, encapsulated, and epitomized yuppiedom. He was the managing director of a small advertising agency and although he had never worked in a large London agency he told clients he had because "they would never be able to find out." He drove an Audi then a Porsche, wore Gucci loafers and Lacoste shirts, was too unfit to play squash so he took up golf, talked about visiting "the estate in Yorkshire" at the weekend, implying that he was visiting his family's country mansion when we all suspected he meant having tea with his old mum on a council estate somewhere in central Sheffield, ate at expensive restaurants, and spent a fortune on for the house he was restoring so that it would be worth five times more than he paid for it and he could sell up, make a bomb riding the property wave, and buy cheaper and larger and renovate another one.

He bought a Purdey shotgun so that he could pay to join the kind of game shoots that people with money are allowed to buy into, he wanted to buy a brand new guitar and saxophone to hang on his wall as decoration, and he would use the word "whom" because he thought it impressed people – but he used it incorrectly so unfortunately it had the opposite effect.

Am I implying that yuppies were all lacking a sense of values? Another of grandma's sayings: they knew the cost of everything and the value of nothing. Yuppies adopted the parts of the culture of wealth which could be purchased and dismissed the rest as anachronistic, irrelevant, and dull.

I admit it; I joined in with some of it. I played squash, joined a gym and went to aerobics classes, and owned my own Alessi kettle. However, coming from a northern, aspirational, socialist, working class background with a mother who taught seven-year-olds and was an artist and dressmaker (for our family) in her spare time, plus a father who had qualified as a piano teacher while working in an office, my sister and I were brought up to think that books, theater, paintings, and musical instruments were the ultimate luxuries. The trappings of middle-class life to which my lot aspired were the artistic ones: things which took time and study to appreciate.

A yuppie "lifestyle" could be purchased immediately; all that was needed was the cash. Encouraged by the political and financial atmosphere, the belief that money was all important gained ground. "Intellectual" was used as a term of abuse. In the United Kingdom, Michael Foot, as leader of the Labour Party, was derided in the tabloid press which decreed that he dressed like a poor person; his achievements were minimalized because he argued against the new approach to putting money above all other measures of success.

However, although yuppies longed to be invited to dine at the country houses of the landed gentry, they would more often spend their weekend at country house hotels, converted after being given up by the titled families who could no longer afford to keep them running. Yuppies tended to hang around with a similar crowd of other yuppies, so their pursuits and purchases would be compared with each other's rather than a group which they would not be invited to join.

From *Snobs*, the novel by Julian Fellowes:

The English upper-classes have a deep, subconscious need to read their differences in the artefacts about them. Nothing is more depressing (or less convincing) to them than the attempt to claim some rank or position, some family background, some genealogical distinction, without the requisite acquaintance and props. They would not dream of decorating a bed sitting room in Putney without the odd watercolour of a grandmother in a crinoline, two or three decent antiques and preferably a relic of a privileged childhood. These things are a kind of sign language that tell the visitor where in the class system the owner places him or herself. But, above all things, the real market for them, the absolute litmus test, is whether or not a family has retained its house and its estates. Or a respectable proportion of them. You may overhear a nobleman explaining to some American visitor that money is not important in England, that people can stay in Society without a bean, that land is 'more of a liability, these days' but in his heart he does not believe any of these things.

This was the era that launched the luxury brands' expansion into the mainstream. Old school exclusivity sold its soul and marketed its brands to the up-and-coming as well as families which had upped-and-come hundreds of years earlier. Brand extension went bananas. Tired British, French, and Italian brands were bought up, brushed down, and turned inside out (literally, in the case of Burberrys) for the new owners to cash in. You may not be able to buy the title, the land, or the Gainsborough portraits of your ancestors, but you can have the silk scarf, the gold watch, the hand-made leather shoes, and the vintage champagne. Yuppies would buy anything with a luxury brand name on it; they lapped it all up! Once

Porsche started marketing sunglasses, the era of the designer name was upon us.

The Official British Yuppie Handbook,[37] an amusing Christmas best-seller of 1984, listed the following:

> Silly things designers sometimes attach their names to:
> Sheets
> Knickers
> Socks
> Legwarmers
> Thermal vests
> Rubbish bins
> Pens
> Handkerchiefs
> Bicycles
> Umbrellas.

Yuppies bought luxury goods for what Vanessa Friedman called "the wrong reasons: status as opposed to quality appreciation."[38] Although no self-respecting yuppie would agree that there was anything wrong with buying status.

The yuppie ideal became fashionable and like all trends, it spread and became influential. I don't think for a minute that people who had previously believed that money was insignificant suddenly began to worship it, nor that the whole of the Western world gave up its ideals and adopted new ones. However, the Thatcher/Reagan promise that everything you ever wanted was available to you and all you had to do was take advantage of what was on offer, was presented in a way which was simple and appealing, so it appealed to those who liked their explanations to be simple. It seemed that whole populations took a step or two towards the new yuppie values. Those who resisted were labeled outdated, hippie, unrealistic idealists.

The *Official Handbook* rewrote the Ten Commandments, yuppie style:

1. Thou shalt have no other gods before thyself – although after thyself, money isn't a bad second.
2. Thou shalt take unto thee only designer labels.
3. Thou shalt be a two income family, for how else canst thou afford all the goodies that God – and the Japanese electronics industry – have blessed us with? (Thou shalt, incidentally, find it better not to wed for thus thou shalt get maximum tax relief on thy thumping great mortgage.)
   ...
9. Thou shalt not kill – although making a killing in the Stock Market is quite acceptable.
10. Thou shalt not covet thy neighbour's Porsche 928S, but shalt do everything short of selling thy spouse into slavery in order to get one too.

The cars of choice amongst those who couldn't afford the Porsches, BMWs, and Mercedes were the souped-up versions of lesser marques: the VW Golf GTi started it, then there was the Peugeot 205GTi, the Renault 5 Turbo, the Ford Escort RS2000; convertible versions were the cars of junior yuppies' dreams.

Flashing your cash became acceptable amongst the young working classes as well as nouveaux-property-riches professionals. Where previously it had been polite to keep quiet in the West about your income and expenditure, money and acquisitions became part of everyday conversation. And as the middle classes married, sent their children to expensive schools, and survived on one income, many found that their mortgages and monthly outgoings swallowed up their gains. Statisticians found that it was the weekly paid workers living in fixed rental accommodation who suddenly had masses more disposable income than their supposed class superiors. In the United Kingdom, comedian Harry Enfield created a character called Loadsamoney who worked as a plasterer, earned a fortune tax free in cash, and drove a Ford Escort "Turbo Nutter Bastard." Enfield's character was brash, boastful, judgmental, and irresponsible and was, to his surprise, adopted as a mascot by working-class southerners who identified with his characteristics. At football matches southern men would wave their wads of cash at northerners yelling "Loadsamoney!" at them. As Londoners were taking advantage of the southern boom, industry in the north was being dismantled, communities ripped to pieces by unemployment, and yuppiedom was severely limited in its geographical effect. Although minor British yuppie flourishes took place later in the city centers and converted warehouses of Liverpool, Manchester, Glasgow, and Newcastle and Gateshead, the wealth was concentrated in the South East, as usual.

To counter the effect caused by his Frankenstein's Monster, Harry Enfield created "Bugger-All-Money" a rather sweet, innocent Geordie comedy character who did not drink cocktails nor own a car, a house, or any means of earning a fortune. He never quite captured the mood of the nation.

19
Work hard, play hard, sell your grandmother

During the 1980s the message which the politicians were transmitting was, "You can have anything you want if you just work hard and make a success of yourself. A growing economy is good for everyone." The message which was being heard was, "We can have anything we want! Why should expensive things be limited to people with posh accents who went to smart schools and poncy universities?" "High taxes are bad for the economy" could be interpreted as, "Paying tax is bad – therefore I shall avoid it where possible."

There was also a negative shift in the kindness spectrum; hardness set in. Although he was apparently intending to be ironic at the time, when the UK's housing Minister Sir George Young said about homeless people, "These are the sort of people you step over when you come out of the opera," people ought to have been appalled by it; instead they were amused.

Education was encouraged but only as a means of getting a good job so that you could work hard, earn lots of money, and enjoy the success and promised happiness which was previously only available to the privileged. Drug dealers claimed to be entrepreneurs, just doing what Mrs Thatcher has told them to do, start their own businesses. Right and wrong took a financial step sideways too; if it made money then it couldn't be wrong, could it?

Of course I am over-simplifying, but in the 1980s there was a terrific shift sideways (which some thought was upwards) in expectations of entitlement. People no longer expected governments to protect them from poverty, but they began to expect far more in terms of what they were entitled to own. Why should they not own a Cartier watch just because they had started life in a dead-end town?

Extrapolating to the corporate level, why should a company choose not to steal someone else's ideas, if it was going to make them a shedload of profit? Someone stole your business idea? Tough! It was a dog-eat-dog world, if you couldn't stand the heat you got out of the kitchen; you were there to work hard and play hard. Clichés abounded. J. R. Ewing in his Texan oilfields was a role model; even he began to look like a bit of a softy compared with the genuine Wall Street moneymakers.

However badly you chose to behave in business in the 1980s and 1990s there was always someone behaving worse than you who was still doing well. Karma had fallen out of fashion; no one seemed to be punished or even mildly disapproved of for trampling their way to the top. Doing the right thing, when the wrong thing would make you more money, was perceived as weak and downright stupid. Altruism, unless it had a concealed financial payoff, in which case it wasn't really altruistic, was pointless.

The results of the 1980s ethics shift are still showing. The *Harvard Business Review* has called for a new direction in management training; one which concentrated not only on finance and marketing but on "soft skills," looking after the employees, re-establishing the lost corporate morality which was swept away in the pursuit of profits in the 1980s and 1990s. Millions of small investors, pension holders, and workers have lost their savings and livelihoods because of the every man for himself attitude which came to power in the 1980s. Doubtless there are places where this behavior is still admired and rewarded; it will take longer than ten years to rinse these bubbles out of businesses.

What relevance does this have to our plot? What influence did this era have on our market for counterfeits? It made it more acceptable to steal business ideas from people who did not have the financial backing to defend them with intellectual property lawyers. It fostered the view that everyone had a right to luxury items. Buying and selling cheap copies of expensive goods became less a matter of right and wrong, of personal morality, but to be considered as a moneymaking or money-saving exercise. Breaking the law to make or save money was considered to be an individual's choice, not simply unacceptable because it was illegal.

The seeds of brand stretching were planted, watered, given a healthy dose of fertilizer, and were already flowering and yielding a profitable harvest. The effects on the brands weren't felt until later. Fragrances flourished, every designer had a label, and every designer label launched a new perfume. If companies could make money by putting their logos on the outside of something which had previously kept itself discretely anonymous, then they would do it. Subtlety was for wimps.

Ironically for the yuppies who believed that they could buy status, "old money" often has a different attitude to spending. European families have been looking after their property for centuries by being frugal in their expenditure. I worked with one seriously wealthy man who inherited his grandfather's Savile Row suits and had the linings replaced in brightly colored silk (which he rather liked to show people) so that they looked as good as new but had saved him a fortune. This delighted him so he told everyone. His suitcases were expensive but built to last a lifetime. A land-owning, old gentleman-farmer I knew was almost turfed out of a smart hotel in Berlin for nor dressing smartly enough; staff assumed that his old leather shoes, his tweed jacket, and his farmer's flat cap indicated that he couldn't afford to stay there. You could spot their discomfort every time he walked through reception. His nephew whispered to me "He's probably got a quarter of a million in his current account; if only they knew." If only they had been polite enough not to let it influence them.

The yuppie decade left its footprints all over the department stores, high streets, and shopping malls of the world. Luxury brands opened their arms and embraced a wider range of buyers who are not intending to give them up.

20
Intellectual property law and international ethics – by a non-lawyer

(Nothing in this chapter should be used as a basis for a legal argument at all. Ever.)

There are thousands of little enterprises around the globe (and some pretty big ones too) who think that it's a great business idea to borrow someone else's business idea and haven't even questioned that it might be intellectual property theft. "Let's copy it before someone else does!" is their cry. It might seem wrong to us, but to them it is just another business opportunity. Lush's boss, Mark Constantine, who is somewhat tired of seeing his products copied to the very last detail, but without the Lush logo, puts it like this: "At school you get expelled for copying. When you leave you can do it as much as you like."

You will be unsurprised to hear that intellectual property law is complicated; this is why companies use specialist IP lawyers, and this brief chapter will not attempt to give advice, merely help to illustrate just how tricky it can be.

In Italy Lush was copied by a small business. They copied all the products that are simple to make – the soap and Bath Ballistics, used all the words from the catalog (translated by Eve Pasquet from my copy) and even scanned in all Lush's own photographs and illustrations. The judge decided that the infringer was to stop using Lush's photographs but the copy and the products were fair game. How wrong is that?

Lush trademarked the word "Rush" for cosmetics use in Japan and Taiwan because the letters l and r and pronounced almost identically in Japanese, as a sound halfway between the Western pronunciation of the two letters. Gucci developed a perfume called Rush then found when they tried to register it that they would be infringing Lush's trademark. Lush granted them a license to use the trademark in Japan and Taiwan, in an agreement which was settled amicably.

In Australia, where Lush had also opened a small business, a company started to use the word "fresh" on all its packaging, which Lush had done from the day it launched in

1995. Lush decided to tolerate and observe the situation, but then the usurper had the audacity to serve an injunction on Lush to prevent them from using the word "fresh," claiming that Lush were copying them. Their injunction was served on Christmas Eve which really irritated Mark Constantine as it was delivered to his door just in time to ruin his holiday. This time the full wrath was unleashed. Lush counter-sued, won and one of the terms of the agreement was that a bunch of ten red roses had to be delivered to Mark's house to say sorry for spoiling Christmas. This inspired the Lush solid bubble bath, Amandopondo, which has a rose bud pressed into the top of each one and is designed as a peace offering. (Amandopondo is believed to mean "I am defeated" in an African language; the name came from a world music CD. It is unlikely to be copied.)

My own work has been copied; having your words stolen is a strange thing and it is almost impossible to prove; the same words must appear in the same order to be able to prove copyright infringement of a writing style. And yet, it is so very obvious to people reading it, even when the word order is changed around a bit. When I first started to write Lush's mail order magazine, *Lush Times*, in 1996, the same style started to crop up in other cosmetics companies' publicity; generally speaking there was very little humor in cosmetics writing before this time. I don't claim to have changed the cosmetics world single handedly as I based my writing style on the Lush creative team's product range; names like God Save the Clean, Rainbow Worrier, and You Snap the Whip Hard Core Body Butter give you the general idea of the way their minds work. It was my job to take the creative team's ideas and write them up and we developed a certain, somewhat flippant, approach which I put into words.

Specifically, the introduction to a rival catalog of cosmetics with natural ingredients was so similar to my style that Lush customers asked if I'd written it for them. I started to wonder if I had! Another copycat sold racks of bath bombs in Lush-style displays, based on wooden fruit boxes which you get in greengrocers. The product names were similar and the writing style was identical, but none of the same words linked up to form an actual copied sentence. Lush worked on an injunction to prevent these people selling copycat products to small shops and department stores. However, in Lush's publicity it was made clear that Lush never sells products through other retailers, so a legal counter-argument could be made that people could not possibly believe the rival's products were Lush's as they were on sale in places which Lush had specifically said it did not supply.

A large high-street cosmetics retailer launched an entire copycat range, as they do with all successful cosmetics brands, to keep their share of that market. The range was not a success; they had invested a great deal in imitating the style, but not in the contents of the products. I openly concede that Lush's functional attributes outweigh its symbolic values, even though the symbolic values are the bit I contribute to. If the attack had come a couple of years earlier, before Lush had its feet firmly under the UK high street dining table, the attackers might have won; as it was, too many people had already tried Lush products and could see, feel, and smell the difference in quality. However, their writing style was basically mine, or a parody of it.

For me, it felt weird to be copied. Reading what were basically my words, on copies of products whose inventors I worked with, made me feel as though all the CCTVs in the store were pointed at me. Somewhere, in a head office in England, people had been sitting around a meeting room table reading my every word then briefing someone else to copy my style deliberately. My feeling was that they should have tried harder to think of something of their own. Why couldn't they use their own brains instead of hijacking mine? For me this was not about money, although intellectual property law tends to measure damages in terms of profits lost or gained; it was about having my own original work stolen by someone else who claims it as theirs. It is like doing your maths homework and having your book stolen by your classmate who copies it out and gets the same mark as you do. It's just not right!

As Mark Constantine says, "I don't mind competition; I like to see good ideas succeed. But I hate being copied. Why can't the lazy bastards have some ideas of their own?"

However, worse things happen in the world of copies and counterfeits. Having my feelings hurt isn't as bad as finding that my malaria drugs don't work, so I shan't witter on about it too much. People who buy fakes assume that it is only massive multinationals making millions who are being copied –possibly they wouldn't even notice! – but often it's people like me who can't do much about it or those working for even smaller companies who have no cash for IP lawyers to defend their work.

Intellectual property rights throughout the world are based on two sources, the "law and economics" approach, and the principles of John Locke, the seventeenth-century English philosopher and leading liberal thinker upon whose writings much of the American constitution was based. Locke reasoned that people should be entitled to enjoy the results of their own labor provided that there is "enough and as good" left over for others to acquire. Intellectual property law therefore gives the creators the right, for example, to earn a fair royalty from their writing, or a share of profits from the manufacture of an invention.

Locke argued against greed: if something had not previously been owned (and this has been extrapolated to include such concepts are new designs, creative works, industrial production methods, and software) then the person acquiring it should take a fair share, not more than he or she can use, and leave plenty for others to acquire later. He aimed for fairness.

European intellectual property law tends towards the Lockean principle. Locke advised following the Law of Nature, which to him meant that no one has the right to harm another in their life, health, liberty, or possessions. (The Law of Nature has since been appropriated by business bullies who take it to mean that the strong will always be able to take advantage of the weak – not what Locke meant at all.)

UK and US IP rights, on the other hand, tend towards an economic approach; if the person who owns a bit of intellectual property is not able to protect it against copying, then there would be no point in developing the idea so that it makes money. This slightly different slant argues that without protection an idea would be copied instantly and others, who had not made the initial investment, would inevitably take the profits.

Locke's approach assumes that in general humankind would agree that it is only right and fair that a handbag designer should earn the profits from sales of his or her design and that other handbag designers should create designs of their own from which to earn a living. Some people would seek to gain by stealing someone else's designs, and the law should be designed to prevent this.

The law and economics approach assumes that given the chance, humankind will steal designs if the punishment for doing so is not sufficiently stringent because the financial rewards will be great; therefore the punishment should be calculated in terms of lost revenue.

Locke's is the moral approach which assumes that most people are fair, and law and economics gives the practical one assuming that most people are.

The French got things up and running early on with the Paris Convention for the Protection of Intellectual Property in 1883, 11 years after the Union des Fabricants was established; this covered inventions, trade marks, and industrial designs. The Berne Convention for the Protection of Literary and Artistic Works in 1886 covered copyright of artistic works: writing, art, and music. In 1974 the United Nations set up an agency which deals with a number of conventions and treaties including the Patent Convention Treaty and the Madrid Agreements concerning trademarks. This is the World Intellectual Property Organization (WIPO).

WIPO and the World Trade Organization work together to implement Trade-related aspects of International Property Rights (TRIPS), which was set up to ensure that the same standards are in place amongst all WTO members. TRIPS extends into new IP areas like information technology issues, databases, downloads – unimaginable when the original team sat down to lunch in Paris 113 years before.

If someone steals your idea what can you do? Absolutely nothing. You cannot trademark, copyright, or patent an idea. You have to show that you would have earned money from it if you are going to claim damages from a person or a business who has taken your original thought and made a profit from manufacturing it.

If you are already making your unique handbag and selling it at local markets, then you notice that an identical design on sale in a chain store, then what can you do? Often the person who is being copied is stuck between a rock and a hard place, as a small company can find IP lawyers prohibitively expensive. Plus, the claimant has to prove that the defendant actually copied him or her, and didn't just think of the idea at the same time, or take inspiration from the same source. The claimant could claim damages or an account of profits. Damages in IP law do not take account of how horrid it feels to have your business stolen; there is no compensation for personal injury. The amount of damages awarded reflects the profit you have lost as a result of your copier selling a product which you could have sold.

If you are taking a weekly stall at a craft market and they are selling in high streets throughout the country, they could argue that you've not lost much money at all; if you were only able to manufacture 50 a week you may only win damages for the profits on that many.

An account of profits treats the case as if the defendant was carrying out the business on behalf of the claimant; if the big chaps were selling 500 a week, then the little chaps could claim the profits on those bags. This may seem promising; however, the big chaps' lawyers are going to argue back.

Why are luxury brands so keen to prove that counterfeiters take business from them and damage their brands? If it can be proved that people who are in the market for a fake would never buy the real thing, then the luxury brand owners' legal claims for damages and an account of profits may be weakened.

Legally, it is wrong to steal the trademark, logo, design, copyright, or anything else that identifies the work of the person or organization whose creativity and own work brought it into existence. To be copied is a violation; on a personal level it feels horrible, as if someone has broken into your home and taken some small things you have kept for sentimental reasons. I'm not normally a vindictive person but I would like the law to include the right to go and give the person who copies your work as good as they gave. Pouring coffee into their filing cabinets or running an electromagnet past their hard drive might do it. As a company, it's as if someone has broken in and emptied the safe. When I was working at the *Guardian* newspaper, thieves stole some carefully selected computers, the hard drives belonging to Tony Ageh's creative team who were developing all the new magazine and online concepts. That was a personal attack, like having their wallets stolen, their handbags emptied all over the pavement, and their minds read.

Counterfeiters steal ideas, but that isn't technically against the law; they also trade on the reputation which other organizations have invested time, effort, and money into developing. They are taking the train without paying the fare. They would probably argue that the train was going there anyway and one more fare doesn't make much difference (as fare dodgers do). That doesn't make it right. One lost train fare raises the cost to the rest of us by a fraction of 1 percent; one sold counterfeit may not make a huge difference to our taxes, but still it makes a micro-difference. Add up enough of them, like 7 percent of world trade, and all of us who pay taxes are paying more as a result. That should be a good enough reason to stop buying the stuff.

The CIA is keen to keep the message as straightforward as possible: counterfeits fund organized crime and terrorism. As ever, it's not that simple. Some do, some don't.

Not all counterfeiters operate outside of the law and by no means all are linked with criminals. Some counterfeiters run legitimate businesses with the exception of the obvious IP part. For example, in Mauritius, wherever you may find a passing tourist, there are shops with Ralph Lauren logos painted on the walls and racks of counterfeits inside. They all claim to be factory outlets although I was told by a businessman in the clothing trade that there is not one single genuine Ralph Lauren factory in Mauritius. I wanted to buy a pair of trousers to replace some I was wearing when I fell over and landed in a muddy puddle; it's difficult to locate anything which is not fake Ralph Lauren or to find a taxi driver who doesn't assume that this is exactly what you want. There is one huge deception going on, but apart from that the "Ralph Lauren outlet shops" are run as legitimate businesses. They are breaking intellectual property law but otherwise are acting within their own legal system, paying their taxes like their neighbors in the next-door shops selling food and handmade furniture.

What about the Moroccan shop selling football kit? Did the owner have the genuine Marrakech team football shirt?

"They cost €60!" he told us, "Not even the real team can

afford to play in real shirts." The counterfeits are made by a clothing business run in the same way as other clothing businesses, just without the official stamp of approval from the Moroccan football association and without paying them a license fee. In Montevideo there is a sports shop which sells shirts labeled "autentico" on the same rack as the obvious fakes. Actually, they were both fakes, but the ones marked as authentic were better quality than the really cheap ones. The closer you look, the more complicated it gets.

Likewise the Chinese counterfeits, which European and American tourists flock to buy when they visit mainland China, are not made or sold by criminals; they are made by low-cost factories where they happen to be breaking intellectual property laws, making a profit, and paying their taxes. It is seen as a fair opportunity. If criminals choose to purchase and import these goods illegally into Europe and the United States it is because they have a ready, willing market for them amongst customers who want Gucci wallets, Dior watches, and Louis Vuitton bags but don't have the money.

Prada have their bags manufactured in China because costs are currently so low that nowhere else in the world can compete on price. Some companies see moving their manufacturing to China, where they can easily be copied, as a huge risk. Others will take the profits and live with the dangers. The Chinese themselves are not interested in owning counterfeits, they want the real thing; they even leave on the price tag to prove to all who see it that they paid top whack for their European designers.

IP lawyers in the United States recognize that they would be fighting a losing battle if they try to stop the kind of copying within the clothing trade that Philip Green described. Diane O'Brien wrote:

> Unlike other products, copyright protection is denied to fashion designers under the US Copyright

Act. Trademarks are available to designs, but it's a fine line between an actual counterfeit and a "creative interpretation."[39]

So although it may be unethical to copy a fashion design, it is not illegal in the United States. So where is this "fine line" to be drawn between ethics, a personal sense of morality, and the law? Wherever you choose to draw it.

21
Expand your market: copy your own brand

In 1959 Pierre Cardin was thrown out of the Paris Chambre Syndicale de la Haute Couture for lowering the tone and making his designs available to the masses with his *prêt-a-porter* collection for Au Printemps. The fashion world was about to change; it followed where Cardin had led. In the twenty-first century Chanel, Yves Saint Laurent, Dior, Lacroix, all the massive names also do ready-to-wear collections. They opened their doors to the middle classes, expanded their business, and enjoyed the rewards.

Since then top brands have followed a trend towards reaching downwards and blessing the peasants with their offerings. When Yves Saint Laurent lipsticks are advertised as "available in larger branches of Boots" you know that the most profitable end of the luxury goods market is available to the masses. They may not be able to afford the frocks, but the lipstick will do for now.

Following *prêt-a-porter*, the next step sideways was "diffusion." Diffusion ranges are often casual wear with the word "jeans" attached to the end of them, DKNY, Armani, and Jean-Paul Gaultier included. Diffusion is what happens when designers bring out a cheaper range, often of less formal clothes, but sometimes of similar styles to their ready-to-wear ranges with less expensive materials, a less intricate cut, fewer embellishments, and consequently, a lower price.

The view is that this broadens the market, it does not bring the more affluent buyers into shops to which they would usually send the hired help; those who can afford it will still buy the top range; those who can't can buy the version with a zero taken off the end of the price. The fashion conscious, frugal consumer can now have a genuine Gaultier or DKNY – with their labels on – without having to search the stores for unbranded copies.

There are two risks to the designer: going downmarket may damage the brand and make it less appealing to the original customers of the expensive items, or the market for the expensive goods may dry up, when people realize they can buy good designs at lower prices.

That is why this kind of brand extension is carefully done; there are two versions of the brand (at least). Those who know are aware that Marc by Marc Jacobs is not the same as Marc Jacobs and Cacharel for La Redoute is not quite Cacharel.

The advantages seem to be outweighing the disadvantages: M. Gaultier, Ms. Karan and the like get a share of the profits for the high street versions of their clothes, instead of seeing their studios' designs ripped-off and repackaged with no chance of reaping the rewards of their labor. They reach a wider range of customers, many of them younger people who might grow up aspiring to the top-of-the-tree version of the brand.

In the United Kingdom, Debenhams department stores have reinvented themselves as a mid-market designer boutiques. Their Designers at Debenhams range includes GS by Gharani Strok, J by Jasper Conran, Butterfly by Matthew Williamson, and Rocha by John Rocha. Coincidentally, one of my neighbors worked as a designer on both the John Rocha and Matthew Williamson ranges. They would visit the name designer's studio and be fully briefed on the range for the season, then create styles based on the designer's forthcoming own range. Instead of rushing to buy the new season's stock, take it to pieces, and ripping it off as other high street retailers are wont to do, they had the luxury of seeing the styles in advance and the pleasure of knowing that they were not unethically making copies of other people's work. Nothing makes it into production without the blessing of the designer whose name is going on it.

The ranges have been hugely successful for Debenhams. Chanel's creative head, Karl Lagerfeld caused much excitement when he put his name to an H&M range too. Lagerfeld has designed for the French catalog retailer, La Redoute, as has Gaultier whose spring/summer 2005 matelot range was delightfully, recognizably of Gaultier's style and made it on to the fashion pages of many a magazine. In the British edition he is described as "Jean-Paul Gaultier, the French couturier" in case the catalog's customers hadn't heard of him. La Redoute's stated aim is to "make the inexpensive desirable" (rather than the other way around).

For followers of fashion in search of the season's look, this trend is a precious gift from the goddess of clothes. An entire Matthew Williamson wardrobe would cost several months wages for the average working woman. If you have a limited budget – and what matters to you is your look of the season – then to head off to the high street or the mall, buy a few bang-up-to-the-moment designs (including the shoes and the bag) put yourself at the forefront of the group you socialize with and not resort to fakes to get the names you want. It's a miracle.

The strategy has worked wonders for Debenhams; what about Rocha, Conran, and Williamson? Customers are free to choose according to their disposable income. If they want the handcrafted silk version with 17 layers of chiffon and individually stitched beads then they can still have one. If they love the look and are happy with the cotton version, run up at a factory with the design printed on, then that's fine too. Does the Butterfly range damage Matthew Williamson's brand? It certainly publicizes his designs to people who would previously have been oblivious. Will his affluent customers stop buying his expensive range because Debenhams sells a cheaper, similar version? I don't think it will, not as long as he continues to make beautiful clothes which set trends of their own.

The Financial Times How to Spend It magazine ran a feature in November 2004 called "Don't we look reasonably fabulous" which asked:

> So you'd like a well-fitted 100 percent cashmere V-neck in this winter's creamy neutrals? Yours for

£25 from Tesco's Finest. Or a sleek, short, black fly-front mac that would not be a disgrace to Helmut Lang or Prada? Sainsbury's brand new TU range has it, at £35. This season's must-have long cardigan, to belt over a Miss Moneypenny skirt but trimly fitted to flatter? Absolutely, at Hobbs £95.

The four women, described as discerning and normally designer-clad, who tested the high street ranges for *The Financial Times*, decided that the disadvantage to high street design bargains is having to trawl the whole high street for the worthwhile buys, a role which women's magazines have adopted for us with a zeal and a passion.

The strategy has not stopped Matthew Williamson's designs being copied all over the place in 2005. The more they are seen in "celebrity" magazines, the more likely that cheap copies are to turn up in chain stories. Tesco's Florence & Fred range (on which my talented neighbor also worked as a designer) has a fabulous copy of a Matthew Williamson dress featured in the press as I write.

Jasper Conran said he believes "that people who don't have so much money should still have nice things" something which LVMH absolutely does not believe about their bags. For their chief, Bernard Arnault, luxury is only truly luxurious if it is also exclusive, by definition excluding the masses from access to it. They create a demand which they refuse to satisfy; so counterfeiters happily hop in to take advantage of the unfulfilled desire which the high end brands create and do it for them.

Follower of the pack

The minute that people in the public eye are spotted wearing new clothes and accessories, an army of copiers flies into action. Once a style has grabbed itself a slice of the free publicity which comes from paparazzi photographs in gossip magazines, there is a demand for it. The original designers' publicity departments often give stars of stage and screen their clothes for nothing, purely for the effect is has on sales when the photographs are published.

An eye-opener for me was asos.com. ASOS stands for as seen on screen. A friend told me that at her company's Christmas party three of the girls from manufacturing turned up wearing exactly the same ASOS dress. The site sells some brands, but mostly its specialism is "in the style of" and "asSeenon" clothing and accessories such as:

- Flower Halterneck Top in the style of Kate Hudson £15
- Butterfly Hair Clip in the style of Sarah Jessica Parker £4
- Jewel Detail Cuff in the style of Beyoncé £5
- Scalloped Mary Jane RT in the style of Scarlet Johannsen £30 [they mean Scarlett Johansson]
- Havaianas Floral Flip Flop asSeenon Giselle £18
- Wide Leather Cuff in the style of Avril Lavigne £7
- LPF Blanchett Hippy Skirt in the style of Cate Blanchett £70

This is not new. The Empress Eugenie of France kicked off an overwhelming trend for purple clothing in Paris in 1857; the following year Queen Victoria picked it up and ran with it in London. In 1856 William Perkin, a British chemist whose works were just up the road from where I live, invented a new chemical dye which turned textiles a stunning shade of purple which he called "mauve" (pronounced "morv" at the time and by my grandmother's generation) after the French flower. After many false starts while he negotiated with fabric manufacturers to have a purple cloth put into production and rival chemists also experimented to produce bright colors of their own, mauve hit the headlines when the Eugenie, encouraged by her husband, Napoleon

III, started to promote French fashion and Lyon silks by wearing the most extravagant examples. Ironically, the French mauve dye was produced by a Lyon chemist who had copied Perkin's color.

Queen Victoria turned up clad in mauve to her daughter's wedding in London in 1858; fashions spread more slowly then; the color was described in newspapers, but it had to be seen in person before it could be appreciated in all its glory. Mauve gloves, ribbons, and whole crinolined dresses were made from it; its first mention in *The Times* was a report of a lost parasol lined with mauve fabric. Mauve was massively popular for around two years after which the trendsetters of the day took to the next batch of bright colors created from new synthetic dyes, but mauve was still the height of popular fashion until 1861. The wealthier dropped the color as it became ubiquitous and even serving girls were seen wearing it. In fact, snobbish horror was proclaimed by the uppers classes who doubted that the working classes ought to be permitted to wear mauve at all. (Do we hear echoes of Burberry, anyone?) Orders came in from as far as Hong Kong. In the meantime Perkin had become a wealthy man as all dyers who wanted to produce the color were obliged to buy the patented chemical from Perkin and Sons. The whole fascinating story is described in Simon Garfield's excellent book, *Mauve*[40] which shows a portrait of the elderly Perkin, a length of mauve silk casually draped over one hand, on the cover. The color pops up every now and again; it is regularly spotted on small children who wear it as part of their private school uniform. A flood of purple blazers and gray flannel spills out daily on to the pavements of Knightsbridge sported by privileged youngsters.

What is it about something new which makes an individual decide, "Wow! that's beautiful, I want one!"? If we knew that we would probably make more of them. Just being new seems to give an article, or in Perkin's case a color, an appeal of its own. Modern commerce depends upon our inability to resist a new trend.

There is a marketing tool which describes the progress of an innovation from its launch to its demise; it was devised by Everett Rogers in 1962 in his book *Diffusion of Innovations* and is called, unsurprisingly, Rogers' Diffusion of Innovation. (Those who are interested in such things will be pleased to know that it follows the classic mathematical bell curve and the segments fit the standard deviation statistical tool.)

It divides all the people who will ever buy a particular product (many, of course, never will) into categories.

The first 2.5 percent are known as innovators; they blaze the trail, take the risks, and probably pay more for their version of any particular product because they want to have it first. (There is an adapted version which divides off the first 0.5 percent as the real ground breakers.)

The next into the market are the early adopters; these take up 13.5 percent of the market.

The early majority form the first big chunk: 34 percent of the market. When you have reached this point, you have already sold your thing to half the market (although how you tell that you've reached this point at the time is an entirely different matter).

You've reached the top of the curve here; market growth starts to slow, although you are still reaching more people.

The next 34 percent form the late majority then the laggards take up the slack with the last 16 percent of your market. At this point, when the slowest of the laggards buys one, that's it; everyone who is going to try it has tried it.

It's a lovely mathematical model and it can illustrate historically what happened to a product, but it cannot predict whether or not your product will be popular, how quickly or how widely it will be adopted by a potential market. However it is useful amongst people who like to look at sales figures and reassure themselves that they were amongst the first 2.5

percent and marketing people use it to perpetrate the business myth of the Product Life Cycle, devised by Theodore Levitt and used by marketers to justify their failures ever since. (See the *Harvard Business Review* May 2005 for details.) Good, strong brands which are looked after by people who maintain high standards of production do not necessarily disappear after a predictable length of time; some will fade away no matter how beautifully they are made because a new product makes them completely obsolete; that's different. Consider the typewriter in the Western world.

What Rogers' Diffusion of Innovation does show is that in order to become successful, a new product or service (like the ability to dye cloth purple) or fashion, has to have its leaders, its innovators. It also shows that there are others who catch on quickly and some who will not even consider new-fangled ideas until at least half the purchasing population has tried it first. The fashion innovators feel instinctively that it is time to move on when they spot that their discovery has been adopted by people they don't particularly wish to impress. Innovators in different product areas are completely different groups of people. Those who download the latest games software may not be the trailblazers when it comes to sporting the latest haircuts. The people who pick up the latest trend in cocktail bars are probably not seeking out and investing in the newest, most cozy pyjamas.

In each field, the 2.5 percent set an example; the 97.5 percent need someone to follow. Do we all have the potential to be original? Probably not.

Stuart Sutherland pointed out the disadvantage of following fashion to its limits in *Irrationality: The Enemy Within:*

> Consider women's fashions, in which the combination of a desire to conform and a desire to excel can lead to some dismaying end products. Fashion trends are usually set by a group that others

admire: depending on the era, it may be the Royal Family, film stars or even – in the sixties when obeisance was paid to youth – the young. Those who lead fashion usually want to differentiate themselves from the multitude that follows them. As the hoi polloi catch up, the leaders try to stay ahead by exaggerating the current fashion and a competition ensures in which exaggeration is in turn emulated by others. This can produce such injurious articles as the stiletto heel, the tight corset, and the crinoline (itself a revival for the third time of the Farthingale). The desire to conform on which the cycle of fashion is based is for the mort part irrational. No-one achieves any of the other attributes of film stars or society women by copying the way they dress. Nevertheless, the extreme and irrational outcomes to which fashion sometimes leads are produced less by individual irrationality than by the interaction of the factors operating within the group, particularly by the influence of conformity and competitiveness.[41]

No, perhaps we can't all blaze the trail, but we could give it a little more thought before we rush to follow.

22
Is creativity cool?

In the early 1990s I was working for a UK national newspaper in the marketing department, organizing exhibitions and events. For amusement I liked to design and knit my own sweaters. I dream a lot of my ideas; one morning I woke up remembering a sweater dream; this one started out as Aran style with cables, then got taken over by a kind of mad knitting virus which turned it into a patchwork for blue and green in many different textures and stitches. I went ahead and knitted it. The editor at the time was a man of few words, none of them wasted. All the junior staff were terrified of being caught alone with him in the lift – quite irrationally as he was a perfectly lovely man – but because we would be struck dumb, trying to think of something reasonable to say which might impress him; generally we would end up either saying nothing at all and looking unfriendly, or blurting out something ridiculous.

I had an editorial elevator moment the first time I wore the sweater to work.

"Nice woolly," he said, to the point. I was so delighted that I completely blew my moment and responded,

"I'll knit you one if you like." He didn't reply. Nevertheless I remain honored that he mentioned it.

The editor of the women's and style pages asked me, "Whose is it?"

"It's mine," I replied. At the time I was unfamiliar with the fashion world's habit of putting the question that way instead of asking, "Who designed it?" or "What make is it?" the way normal people do. It's a code they use amongst themselves to weed out amateurs like me.

She sighed.

"Who designed it?" she asked with a smidgen of resignation at being made to work harder than expected to get an answer to a simple question.

"I did," I said. This was still apparently the wrong answer.

"Well, where did you get the idea?" she asked, refusing to give up her quest for the original source material.

"From the inside of my own head," I replied. At this point the sweater became suddenly uninteresting to her. If the idea was not from a recognized designer, a copy or replica or "inspired" by someone she had heard of, then it slid off the edge of her attention span into fashion oblivion.

In 1969 Jerzi Kosinski's novel *Steps* won the American National Book Award for fiction. In 1977 somebody retyped it and submitted it for publication with no title and a false name to 14 publishers and 13 literary agents. Not a single one of them recognized it and all of them rejected it. Without the author's name no one noticed that it was any good (possibly no one bothered to read it). Authors are brands too.

We are much more willing to accept a recommendation, to buy a product, or take advice, from a source we trust and a name we know. If my sweater had been designed by someone the editor had heard of or a small design studio staffed by recent London School of Fashion graduates, then its conformity (and mine) to nice safe parameters would have made it (and me) a good deal cooler than my sweater and I were judged to be by the fashion expert. (The editor made his judgment on an entirely different basis – simply on whether he liked it or not.)

People to whom we go for advice on the latest trends are known as mavens. A maven is a person whose guidance you follow in matters of taste and style and sometimes for technical advice too. (A computer maven is a useful person to know.) The word was first used in this context by Linda Price, Professor of Marketing at the University of South Florida in the late 1980s. Mavens can be friends who happen to be experts in certain fields, the ones who seem to sniff out what's warm and what's hot. They can be professionals who are paid for their expertise. People with budgets may call them in and hire them by the hour; the rest of us read their magazine columns or their blogs.

The fashion pages' "in and out" columns are written by professional mavens. Others include personal shoppers and stylists who choose clothes and create looks for famous people and television programs.

Advertisers pay famous people to become mavens for their brand, but as we've said, sometimes that works and sometimes it doesn't. If an Olympic athlete becomes spokesperson for the shoes in which she just won the 100 meter sprint, that rings true; if she suddenly starts to appear in advertisements for watches and handbags, we know she's cashing in on her 15 minutes of fame.

In the late 1990s Nike were carrying out focus group research to find school mavens.[42] They had discovered that an entire school could be turned on or off a sports clothing brand by one leading figure. If the school maven wore Nike, so did the other 999 pupils; if she owned Pumas, so did they. The maven decreed what was cool and what wasn't.

Some say that the quest for "cool" kills creativity. When a group is so influenced by the opinion of others – because coolness truly exists only in the eyes of the people one hopes to impress – that their behavior is dictated by the search for acceptance, then taking a chance with an unknown brand is too risky. It's an interesting thought, but it probably says more about the judgment of the friends of the person who proposed the theory than the essence of "cool" itself.

Being cool can be overrated. At which point did it become cool not to understand maths? For several years I taught a postgraduate course to marketing people in which they had to learn what a budget was, what to do with one, how to calculate a price in order to make a set profit, and what would happen if they sold less than they were expecting. The French, Spanish, Italian, German, and Dutch students had absolutely no problem with this, but most of the British were less than useless. There must be British companies losing masses of money because they believe that to make a 20 percent profit margin you add 20 percent to the costs.

The shift away from understanding percentages has allowed banks to market credit cards on the basis of their color scheme and get away with charging a higher APR. As a group, our financial skills have fallen in tandem with our financial responsibility and planning.

One of the Slow Living Movement's theses, which was born in Italy but adopted and adapted to suit the bustling United States and United Kingdom, is that we all work so hard these days that we leave no time for genuinely creative thought, not the real groundbreaking stuff. (Read Tom Hodgkinson's *How to be Idle* for details.) One of my favorite tales from Economic History O level was about James Brindley, the Duke of Bridgwater's engineer, the man who created the Grand Cross Canal, a miracle of advanced engineering for his day; in the twenty-first century we probably no longer have the ability to recreate his work. When he had a huge obstacle to negotiate (like how to get a canal from one side of a range of hills to the other) he would take to his bed and think until he came up with an answer.

How would your boss feel if you suggested that as a solution to a pressing problem? Is it any wonder that companies copy each other's ideas? How can we justify taking time to clear some space in our busy heads and timetables for ideas of their own to appear. If there are mavens around us who can supply us with ideas then let's have them! There are organizations that have noted the lack of time available for generating inspiration and built businesses on it; trend spotters collect ideas from individual mavens and post them on their websites in regular trend reports for businesses to borrow. Take a look at trendwatchers.com and their maven site springspotters.com:

The Springspotter Network consists of more than 4,000 global business and marketing-savvy *spotters*, who recognize a new business idea when they come across one. A vibrant mix of *cool hunting, new business ideas and trend spotting*, findings are sent to our team of researchers and editors, and may be featured in newsletters like Springwise New Business Ideas or trendwatching.com.

If you join Springspotters, you'll receive points for each accepted submission, which can then be redeemed online for *cool gifts*, delivered to wherever you live on this globe. To see what gifts your observations and findings may net you, check out our gift page. And there are more ways to *earn points*: you'll be presented with a full overview after you sign up.

Cooldom delivered in a time-saving package! How tempting. Let's borrow everyone else's creativity all nicely packaged for businesses to keep ahead of the pack and only a couple of steps behind the people with time to think for themselves.

Copying is part of human nature; it's one of the ways that we learn. Social groups are defined by it; imitation is flattery, some of the time. At what point does copying a new idea transgress the unwritten rules? It's great when your friends admire your style and adapt it to their taste; it's bloody annoying when they turn up in the exact same shoes and top to the same party. Seeing a sweater in blue and deciding to knit your own version in pink may be OK for most; deciding to manufacture 1,000 of them and sell them cheaper is less cut and dried.

The counterfeiting industry encourages ingenuity amongst tax evaders and intellectual property law breakers, but "That's nice; I shall copy it!" doesn't really count as genuine creative thought. Is the huge market for fakes the result of a lapse in creativity amongst both the people who make them and the people who buy them? Maybe it's just laziness; we simply cannot be bothered to come up with new ideas of our own.

23
Handbags at dawn

Who or what pulls the strings which make us buy what we buy? How strongly are we influenced by brand identities? All our previous experiences of a brand connect up those handy shortcuts in our brain's wiring so that we don't have to stop to think before we make a decision; it's already made for us. I think we should do some work to unravel our hotwired consciousness, put in some time to time on reassessing our ready-formed opinions, so that when a brand pulls one of our strings, it doesn't necessarily link straight to the nerve which operates our enable-purchase reaction.

While I was researching this book, I decided to go shopping for a bag, one I would find useful and that I thought was attractive, without looking at the labels first to influence my judgment. I wanted to test myself to see how easily I am impressed by brands and if I could find a useful item, which I chose for myself, without all the brand messages I have learned in the past pressing the buttons and ringing the bells in my brain telling me, "That one! That one!" I went to TKMaxx because any fool can go straight to Liberty and choose a wonderful bag; their buyers have already selected the world's coolest, most beautiful, and often the most expensive bags so that people with the money can shop there and know that no one anywhere, ever, could call them uncool. On a normal (pay)day I would have gone to Liberty, but that would have been cheating. TKMaxx stocks brands of all persuasions; that would be a true test.

My favorite bag was red leather; it had interesting features: side pockets, zips and inner pockets, and a wide strap. It was wide but shallow and flat. I was drawn to its unusual shape, but rejected it on the grounds that I could not fit a book into it. I always have a book with me, usually two, one for reading and one for writing in, plus a pencil case full of interesting and varied writing implements. With this bag, I would have to carry a second one for literary pursuits. I checked; it was a Mandarina Duck bag, one of my favorite brands for its amazing designs, definitely a fine bag, but perhaps it had made its way to TKMaxx discount land because it didn't sell in sufficient quantity, most probably owing to its lack of book capacity.

Why do I like Mandarina Duck? I first encountered them in Paris (one point) in a small, trendy street in Le Marais (another point). I own only one of their bags but I love almost every one I see (three points). Their shops are lovely (another point) and the bags' styles are new and unusual (two more points). My friend Marco di Gregorio, maven extraordinaire, owns their bags (about seven points) and I have to stop and think twice before I buy one because they are average to highly priced (two points for exclusivity). That's my experience of the Mandarina Duck brand. I see the label and all these things make me feel positively towards it.

I chose a small, purple, woven fabric backpack with two black leather shoulder straps. My physiotherapist had made me promise never to hold the phone between my ear and shoulder and not to hang a bag from one side of my body following a neck and shoulder injury acquired from years of misuse at the computer. This bag had three pockets (I like my pockets) and the center one was book-sized. Ideal. It turned out to be made by Dents, the glove people and although I had promised not to be brand led, I was pleased to think that I had bought something which carried an old, respected name (on the inside only) to reassure me that it was well made.

The second item in my haul was a black satin evening bag, embroidered with big, bright, multicolored flowers. The two handles were as big as bracelets, metal hoops which I can slip over my wrist; they click just like jewelry does. It feels as if I'm wearing it, not carrying it. I can get a phone, pen, lipstick, keys, small notebook, and credit cards in it; a stonkingly good evening bag, at a low price. I had never heard of the manufacturer. I do wonder if it is a copy of an expensive bag with which I am unfamiliar. I half expect to bump into someone who knows much more than I do about fashion who will say, "Oh, is that a copy of the 2003 autumn season Givenchy?"

Another bag I bought during my "follow your heart and ignore the branding" research came from a market stall near my home. I chose the bag I thought was the nicest; it was blue cotton with red trimming and embroidered flowers, plus tiny glass beads hand-sewn on. That day, I also bought a book on handbags; if I was going to investigate the second largest counterfeit market, I thought I ought to study the originals. So, imagine my surprise, as the cliché goes, to find that my bag was an exact copy (embroidery, not shape) of a Fendi baguette bag from 2001. Now I found this very annoying. I would happily have used my pretty £20 bag but I didn't want anyone to think I was trying to look like a sad person who wanted a real Fendi but couldn't afford one, so had to buy a copy. Then I found it even more annoying to discover that I valued the opinion of people I don't actually know.

The most interesting bag bought during my quest was from the sub-Post Office near my house. It is shaped like a Fendi baguette (long and thin) with a buckle which looks a bit like their two capital Fs logo, but it is embroidered with tiny glass beads which make up the Burberry check; it is a complete mongrel of a handbag: "inspired" by almost every popular style from the end of 2004.

The most outrageously derivative bags, "homage" to the luxury brands at the time, turned out to be by the Jennifer Lopez brand, JLo, who not long before that had appeared in Louis Vuitton press advertising, and Baby Phat, Kimora Lee Simmons' brand. Businesswoman and former model Kimora Lee calls herself the world's biggest collector of Louis Vuitton, but couldn't resist marketing some B-list bling versions of her own. I bought those just to prove they existed. I found it fascinating that the organizations to which these two women attach their names could be so shameless about their "inspiration."

So did I succeed? Did I end up with bags that I wanted and no one else influenced me to buy? Did I make a purchase free of having my strings pulled? Probably not.

I once bought a bag from a market in Marrakech. It is made from red leather (two points) and beautifully embroidered with silk flowers (two points), with a red silk cord and it didn't cost much (two more points). You can't get a book in it (minus one). When I showed it to our group guide, Hassan, he wept with laughter. Apparently, this was the kind of bag Berber shepherds use to keep their Berber sandwiches in when they're up in the Atlas mountains looking after their sheep. He'd never seen anything as funny as a woman carrying a Berber shepherd bag. (Picture a pin-striped suited business man carrying a little gold evening purse for his pens and credit cards.) All the same, Berber shepherd bags had made it into London shops by the following spring. Hassan's view and my view of the bag were formed by somewhat different experiences and as a result I'd bought it. I think I made a great purchase and he's probably still telling the story to his mates over a tagine supper.

None of us likes to feel that we are being manipulated; we think we read advertisements and editorial for information. I'd wager a month's shoe money that we all think that we have our own individual style and that our purchasing decisions are hardly influenced by anyone; we all decide for ourselves, accepting and rejecting according to our own judgment. We don't care what other people think! That said, I just looked at one of the JLo branded bags I had bought and decided that I couldn't bear to be seen with it. (What would people think? They'd think I was the kind of person who buys bags encrusted with fake diamonds and smothered in fake fur! Yikes!) In an interesting twist, one of my best chums, a cinema maven and handbag lover who is free from the constraints of string-pulling brand identity in the accessory market, really loved one of the JLo bags, the one in tweed and fake fur. I happily gave it to her, disappointed at my own shallowness, and glad that it had found itself a home where it would be appreciated.

What would it be like to go back to using our own imaginations and our own judgment and deciding for ourselves what we want to wear? Even better, we could learn some skills and make up our own designs. We rely on our friends, our favorite magazines, and our in-groups, all the people we meet at work or socially, for guidance and influence, but we still like to think we make our own decisions, free of external influences and the opinions of others.

As Brian's mum said in the film *Monty Python's Life of Brian*:

"You're all individuals, aren't you?"

And we all like to think we'd be the lone voice who cries, "I'm not!"

24
Mavens and magazines

In the marketing community it is widely accepted that the best form of publicity is "word of mouth," meaning that someone you know and trust, one of your mavens, recommends something to you. One guerrilla marketing tactic involved getting products into the hands of the right people, the ones with a lot of influence amongst a large group of people, the mavens in that particular market. This is why you get free samples of chocolate or moisturizer or cinema tickets. The next most effective publicity is a mention in the media. People treat their favorite magazines rather like their friends, and if one of the magazines whose advice they trust (often with a certain amount of skepticism in these media-conscious days) tells them something is a good buy, they'll be more likely to buy it. Even more effective as a marketing coup is to have a famous person reported in the press as using your product or shown wearing your style or carrying your handbag of the moment.

In 1996 I met journalist and style commentator Peter York for long enough to have a proper chat. He told me that when Swatches were first launched, his friend and publicity queen Lynn Franks (on whom the *Absolutely Fabulous* character Edina is loosely based, allegedly) was the woman in charge. She sent him one in the post as a gift, with a note to say she thought he might like it. Later in the week he got a call from a journalist asking if he was wearing a Swatch. "Yes, I am," he said, and the next thing he knew, he was reported in the press as a fan of Swatches, something along the lines of, "Style guru Peter York is already wearing one." Ms Franks had set him up, but he forgave her because he admired the way that she had gone about it.

These days we often call people we copy "role models." It sounds nicer somehow than merely calling them those people we like to copy. It legitimizes it, although its effect has been that people imitate not only the admirable actions of a person they admire, but also their dress sense and sometimes their whole way of life too. Since the launch of *Hello!*, the celebrity magazine market has gone bananas; again, this is not a new thing, but with new production and distribution methods the effect is broader and faster. The rich and famous have been copied since the time of the industrial revolution, when people started to question their preordained place in society and encouraged by the successes of class escapees, began to aspire to the lifestyles of the well-off.

Advertising comes third on the list of desirable publicity, however advertising is the one over which the brand guardians have control (usually).

During the mayoral election campaign for London's first elected mayor Ken Livingstone's campaign team came up with the slogan:

Ken 4 London.

This was immediately altered by a rival faction to:

Ken 4 London 0.

This goes to show that if you are going to put your advertising on a hoarding in reach of a ladder, a long arm, and a spray can, then you have to be particularly careful.

If advertising didn't work, it would all be canceled. Advertisers argue that their work cannot force someone to buy something; this is true. But what it can do is to inform people that something they might like is available. Advertising is not inherently evil. If you want to sell your car or rent out your spare room, you stick an ad in the local paper. Advertising agencies do the same thing with bigger budgets. Lying in advertisements is evil; telling half truths is nasty and likely to reflect badly on you, like suggesting that the lavatory brush with built-in foam cleaner can actually get your loo completely clean. No one will buy a bad product twice.

For a marketing team, everything falls into place beautifully when advertising is accompanied by recommendations
in editorial news and features sections, followed by a report
telling readers that a rich or temporarily famous person uses
their item; this is just about perfect synergy for a brand.
Wealth and fame currently endow people with an artificial
status, and brands take advantage because we have somehow come to accept that that rich, famous people have better
taste than the average and give them far more credit for their
taste than they rightly deserve. In the words of La Rochefoucauld, "The world more often rewards signs of merit than
merit itself."

They have more choice, this is true, but often they have
been "Yorked," given something for nothing so that they can
be used to impress the impressionable – and I definitely
include myself in that group although I am doing my best to
stay objective. No matter how analytical and media-savvy
we think we are these days, we are still buying stuff! We just
like to think that the stuff we buy is a lot cooler than the stuff
other people buy!

What do magazines tell us to buy? They do not tell us to
buy counterfeits, but you would be forgiven for thinking that
they condone it. (The italic text is mine not theirs.)

New magazine:

> In the changing room with Rachel Stevens. The
> former S Clubber looks effortlessly casual, yet
> polished to perfection – and you can too!
> The petite pop princess always looks groomed
> and gorgeous – *so steal her style.*"[43]

Eve magazine has a "Catwalk crib sheet" to show wily readers how to copy the look with high-street garments and
accessories, and a *"Steal her style"* on how to recreate a
celeb's look:

How to wear ... New Vintage. It's a little bit 60s, a little bit 70s, with a liberal dash of boho chic thrown in. So how's a girl supposed to work that lot into her wardrobe? Just *follow our foolproof cheat sheet.*[44]

Their "speed shopping" feature on jeans was captioned: "Of course they're designer!" sub-titled: "And who's to know the difference, with our guide to the new cult jeans and their purse-friendly copycats?"[45]

B magazine's "Style stalker" takes a current "celeb," deconstructs her outfit and advises readers on how to replicate it for a fraction of the price.

Marie Claire's "Get the look for less" is fascinating because it copies its own styling. A fashion shoot featuring the likes of Louis Vuitton, Miu Miu, Dries van Noten, Eley Kishimoto, Alberta Ferretti, and other aspirational (costly) designers is followed up in the same issue with pages showing the cheaper alternatives, like sandals for £45 instead of £265. It is a useful service for readers who can't afford the real thing, but you can't help feeling that it might irritate the ones who can. Perhaps they are reading *Tatler*, which does not debase itself by scrabbling around hunting out cheap alternatives for readers who can afford the originals.

Now magazine has "I want it, I need it, I've got to have it," which shows how to copy looks; if the high-street press offices have not sent in their own styles, with a photographic reference to the original for the magazines to use, then I will eat my pink pashmina. Readers are advised that the black, ribboned, Versace dress which Catherine Zeta-Jones wore for the Elizabeth Arden Provocative Woman advertisement "is no longer available to buy. You can still look like a star in this similar dress from Freeman's, £45, 8–16, also available in cream."

Halle Berry's Matthew Williamson dress which she wore to the *Catwoman* preview cost £1,000 and is sold out but ASOS.com do a similar design for £35.

Marie Claire also runs a "Spree v steal" section which compares a £170 straw hat with an almost identical £4 version from George at Asda, a cheap but trendy designer line only on sale at the UK supermarket (now owned by Wal-Mart). The similarity between the Michael Kors silk chiffon dress at £1,380 and the Etam polyester version £35 was remarkable, but I'm sure that *Marie Claire* wouldn't want to imply it had actually stolen the design.

Elle's "cheat chic" recommendation shows a £35 version of a £1,026 Chloé bag.

How about *Bliss*'s "They've got it ... we want it! Go get it" page? Kate Moss, Angelina Jolie, and Christina Aguilera are shown in their leather jackets, then *Bliss* directs its readers to a £69.99 version from H&M. They have them, we should have them too!

My favorite has got to be the *Red* magazine section entitled "What a (great) rip off!" which features a Missoni dress and its high-street counterpart at £45. The clothes are identical, apart from the quality of the fabric and finish. The idea has been stolen, unashamedly.

Even *Vogue* has run a "Cheap chic" supplement: one of its recommended buys was a £10 military style jacket from Primark, the bargain store which has finally been outed as the fashionista's guilty secret.

I admit to having selected them carefully, but the impression from these features is that it is perfectly reasonable to steal other people's ideas, copy their designs, and generally get your fashion look at all costs. Vanilla Paris, a bag shop which copies expensive signature styles like the Hermès Birkin and Kelly styles, gets a mass of press coverage in the "get their look" sections. These bags are copies, not counterfeits; they do not attempt to pass themselves off as Hermès by stitching on a label.

Copying may not be illegal, but is it right? Magazines reckon it's fine.

What do their readers think? Is there such a huge differ-ence between buying a bag which looks just like the real thing and buying one which looks just like the real thing, including the logo? So what if they crossed a fuzzy line and went for what the Internet ads calls "authentic counterfeits?" Is that so much worse? Legally, yes. But when the US govern-ment officially allows its citizens to import one every 30 days, then perhaps it is understandable that people desperate to have the look they want find the guiding signals less than clear when they read their chosen media.

The currently celebrated, who perpetuate their own popu-larity by padding the pages of scandal rags and gossip mags, are able to influence the hundreds of thousands of readers who also aspire to be famous for doing nothing much. Their collective penchant for luxury branded goods has multiplied the shopping public's awareness and desire for these clothes and accessories by a factor far greater than the supply. One strange counterfeit story emerged when the United King-dom's most famous footballer's wife was said to have bought a counterfeit Louis Vuitton bag; she was shown in gossip magazines carrying the design, but Louis Vuitton were reported to have issued a statement saying that they had not sold it to her and she had not been on the waiting list. As LV bags are only sold through their own shops and concessions within department stores, they would know. There is a woman who can have any fashion item she wants; when denied something, she is said to have acquired the closest possible thing, an "authentic counterfeit."

Whether it was true or not, the story spread, allowing aspirational shoppers worldwide to say to themselves, "Well, if it's OK for her, it's OK for me!"

25
Shopping: a new world hobby

One spring afternoon I took a break to sit in the sun drinking tea and eating chocolate with my neighbor and her aunts. The chocolate came from the 69th floor of the Landmark Tower in Yokohama, which has lifts which get you up there in 45 seconds. At the top there is a fantastic view – although one of my friends was up there on a cloudy day and thought they had stupidly put frosted glass in the viewing windows – plus a café and a souvenir shop. What a souvenir shop it is! It has its own cartoon character, Blue Dal, a Dalmatian dog with blue spots; you can buy Blue Dal stickers, postcards, t-shirts, candy-coated chocolates like Smarties or M&Ms but only in shades of blue, and rolls of self-adhesive decorative tape which tells stories of the different ways in which Blue Dal keeps gaining and losing his spots. They are all beautifully designed and of good quality.

Other branded souvenirs include a range of goods with a seagull symbol, a small girl with red shoes, the harbor bridge, a graphic of the tower itself, an art deco style ship, and a brick wall, based on Yokohama's Red Brick Warehouse, a converted early nineteenth-century port building which has also been turned into an eating and shopping center. I probably spent more time choosing gifts in the store than I did looking out of the windows, and I brought home seven bars of chocolate and two tins of mints because the packaging designs were so beautiful.

According to my friend Angela, who thinks it was Julian Barnes who first wrote about this, when people visit an art gallery they spend on average more time deciding which postcards to buy than they do looking at the pictures. When I think about recent visits to Baltic in Gateshead, the Hayward, and both the Tates in London, I have to confess that I probably did just that. For shoppers uninterested in the actual art, it's well worth going to the Museum of Modern Art (MoMA) shop in New York without bothering with the gallery at all, because it's such a brilliant shop full of truly beautiful things designed specially for MoMA. The same is true of the London Transport Museum shop in Covent Garden, the Design Museum near Tower Bridge, and the V&A in South Kensington. Museums have worked out that it is bad business to make people go all the way through the museum before reaching the shop or the restaurant. As long as the shop sells things that are consistent with its brand identity and the carrier bags have big logos on them to act as advertising, then why not take the cash? It's a bit like buying a Chanel lipstick when you can't afford a couture ball gown; perhaps you can't have an actual Ming dynasty Chinese vase, but you can buy a lovely ceramic by a modern craftworker whose work may be that valuable in 100 years' time, or a postcard.

Shopping has become recreational: there is the old-fashioned kind of shopping which involves going out with a purpose to buy something you want or need, and there is new shopping, browsing for the fun of it. Years ago there used to be window shopping: visiting smart shops to look at things you couldn't actually afford. That was a bit like going to see the exhibits in a museum before the days when you could buy reproductions in the shops attached. (I could never see the point of it.) On an Internet forum recently I was writing about the idea of giving up shopping, and I was asked by an American, did I mean "buying" or "shopping?" To me, they are the same thing; shopping means spending money. I now appreciate that there exists a whole different level of shopping – going out enjoying yourself just looking at things –which I hadn't realized existed.

For the last 50 years, shopping has been presented to us as a means of making ourselves happy; if we own stuff we will achieve our goals, be equipped to display the trapping of success, even if we have borrowed the money to get the trappings, hoping that the success will follow later and get us out of the financial sticky mess we've landed ourselves in.

There are "chic-lit" books about the trials of being a shopaholic, but shopaholic, like chocaholic is used as a light-hearted term; it does not imply that a person has serious problems, just silly little ones. The HBO television series *Sex and the City* gave the ultimate stamp of approval to the turn of the century shopping culture. The program's stylist could launch a designer by placing Carrie, Samantha, Miranda, or Charlotte in a meticulously selected dress. When Carrie had it pointed out to her that she had spent $40,000 on shoes, enough to have paid the deposit on her New York apartment, it could have been a significant moment of awakening for shoe shoppers of the Western world, but it was solved in a flash when Charlotte sold her expensive diamond engagement ring to raise the funds. (So that's OK then.) In real life, there are too few Charlottes and too many credit-card-funded shoe collections. *Sex and the City* was fiction but it wasn't fantasy. One reason it was so very successful was that real women recognized aspects of themselves in the fab four. Carrie lied about giving up smoking; Charlotte accidentally married a man in thrall to his mother; Miranda worked silly hours and tried to look after her son alone; Samantha bought a fake Fendi baguette bag from the dodgy man selling them from the back of his car and regretted it later.

Millions of women thought they could be like that too: shoppers and proud of it!

In his book *Why We Shop* Professor Jim Pooler says that exposure to mass media has raised our expectations for material goods beyond all reason. He reckons that the desire to acquire has become a real psychological need but he also seems to think it entirely reasonable that happiness will come from fulfilling those needs, and recommends strategies for retailers to create more of them (both strategies and needs). In the 1980s we could watch the TV series *Dallas* and covet the cars, clothes, and cash, but anyone with a brain could see that all it brought with it was alcoholism, infidelity, misery, and the occasional attempted murder. Perhaps we imagine that if we had the money it would be different for us; we'd manage it properly and we'd be very happy indeed. At the very least it's worth buying a weekly ticket for the lottery just to see what it would be like if we gave it a go.

So we read our favorite magazines and watch television programs which show us more things we could buy. Professor Jim doesn't seem to think there's anything wrong with wanting more and more stuff, as long as we have the means to buy it. He believes that it satisfies real needs and makes us happier to own it all. I don't agree.

In the height of the Thatcher/Reagan capitalist greed-is-good era I was sitting on the waterfront in Hong Kong watching the ships go by. A small boy came up to me and asked to read my fortune. It wouldn't cost anything, he said. He didn't seem to understand the word "no" so eventually I caved in because it seemed that the only way to get rid of the annoying little twerp was to agree to go along with it.

He got out a piece of folded paper and asked, "What do you want from life?"

He wanted an instant answer so, taken by surprise, I mumbled, "To be happy."

"Rich!" he declared.

"No, happy," I said.

"Yes," he said, speaking to me slowly as if I was a complete idiot, "rich!" There was absolutely no way to explain to him that in my mind the two could exist separately.

He wiggled the bits of folded paper, told me I would be rich and asked for money.

"You said it was free," I said.

He tutted with impatience and explained that this had been before he had given me an auspicious reading and now he wanted money for it.

I looked up the happy phrases in my dictionaries of slang and proverbs:

> Happy as a sand boy.
> Happy as a clam. (US).
> Happy as Larry. (Australian).
> Happy as a pig in shit. (UK, nineteenth century).

Nowhere is there a phrase which says, "Happy as a rich person," except ironically.

Yet during the 1980s this was the political message that was peddled in the Western world. Work hard, reap the rewards of your labors and you will be happy with your Porsche, your big house, your luxury holidays, and your artifacts.

In the 1990s there was a move towards accepting that consumer goods couldn't give you everything you wanted. The modern proverb, "No one ever went to the grave wishing they had spent more time at the office," was invented, although I can't find out who said it first. People who had worked ridiculously hard found themselves jobless as their corporation was taken over by a larger corporation, and began to see that hard work could not absolutely guarantee material success.

Now, we do try to retain some common sense in the way we spend our hard-earned pennies. Even though we may splash the cash now and then we always have a reason to justify it:

> "Well, it was my birthday!"
> "I deserve a treat now and again."
> "I just can't resist beautiful things."
> "It's such good quality."
> "It will last me forever."
> "You can't really economize on things like shoes, can you?"
> "It's so much warmer than artificial fibers."

"It's my money and I earned it."
"I can't help being extravagant."

Shopping is now part of our culture; the anti-shopping movement is having an effect, but when retailers look at their annual accounts they still smile. Those who are singing the song about how things can't buy you happiness are being joined by an ever-growing chorus: get out of the rat race, adopt a simpler life, downshift, take a less materialistic and more spiritual approach to life; it sounds beautifully appealing. We need more time and space, not more money or things. (And there are plenty of ecologically sound things we can buy to help make this happen!) Word is that the most environmentally sound car is the one you already own, but we are encouraged to scrap the old one and buy one with a catalytic converter. We are encouraged to jettison our old stuff and buy new stuff which doesn't exploit peasants or children or use heavy metals. Only the seriously left field actually suggest that we should buy less!

Yoga suddenly grew popular in the late 1990s in the United Kingdom, and with it came a market for yoga mats, bags, blocks, clothing, and belts. It got so huge that Nike started to sell branded yoga mats. Puma even started selling yoga shoes, when any yoga teacher will tell you that yoga is done barefoot. As a yoga teacher, who happened to bump into a Nike employee at a parcel depot, I was invited in the to London HQ to have a look at their new range of yoga clothes. It wasn't suitable for yoga – too baggy; it would all fall into the wrong places when people stood on their heads – although their running clothes will do nicely. They had made a range of clothes for people who liked the idea of doing yoga but didn't actually have time, so instead they could hang around the house looking as if they might do yoga, one day soon. Delay the downshifting, just do the shopping ready for the day the downshifting starts.

I worry that people will only join in the worldwide

demonstrations on No Shopping Day if they have managed to get a suitable outfit.

We are interrupted and disturbed by invitations to shop. Even while I type, e-mails arrive constantly to invite me to visit shopping websites. Magazines and newspapers show me lovely things with which I can improve the quality of my lifestyle. It has become fashionable to admit that we love going out to buy things, and the size of our overdraft is a sign of our involvement in modern life. Our shopping wisdom is another way to show off how well we cope with the pressures of modern living; we are as putty in the hands of luxury brands. If we can't have the real one, the fakes are available, on sale in full view of the passing police, on market stalls everywhere. If they were illegal, surely they wouldn't be there, so it's fine to buy them, isn't it?

26
Maintenance and desire

Whatever people have bought, no matter how expensive it was, unless they decide they have made a big mistake (post-purchase dissonance) and take it straight back again, there is a common strand of thought: they got good value for it. Post-purchase assonance, the feeling that you have done the right thing in buying something, is part of decision making and is well known in the part psychology/part marketing field known as Consumer Behavior. We cannot go through life doubting the sense of all our past decisions; we don't have time for that. Unless we have made a terrible error, we tend to post-rationalize, tell ourselves that we made the right decision and then happily jog along with our lives.

What gives value for money? Some illuminating views on what makes a purchase good value came tumbling out of the research. We were asking about clothes and accessories but you can feel free to extrapolate.

> "Anything I like is worth the money in some sense."

> "Good quality, long lasting."

> "They are made well and will last. Style is outstanding."

> "If something is well made and will last I don't mind paying full price for it. For example, I LOVE my Ugg boots, they kept my feet toasty warm all last winter while I was walking my dog and taking her to the park."

> "Excellent comfort and quality"

> "Value for money, i.e. quality = price."

"It's not necessarily the whole brand, it's that I see something I want and have to have it there and then because it's gorgeous. If I've got the space on the credit card I'll get it."

"They are good quality. The clothes I pay a lot for are generally functional – i.e. for cycling or trekking etc. I need them to be 'up to the job' and do what's required of them."

"They last and I feel good wearing them."

"Again, if I like it, I'll buy it for cut, fit, quality more than brand name."

"Quality."

The reality is that very few of us buy non-essentials only for the value that they offer us; we may say "it was really good value" to justify a purchase, but only those of us who are strapped for cash and have no choice, or truly care not a jot, actually write with unbranded ballpoint pens on 99p pads of lined paper and carry our belongings in free bags from the local supermarket. Having said that, I did know one chap whose frugality was his hobby; he built his personal brand identity by giving away books he was bored with as birthday presents (wrapped in used paper bags from grocery shops), hand-sewing elbow patches on his worn sleeves, and making his own lampshades from used financial computer printouts and paperclips. In general, our opinions are influenced by our impressions of a brand's identity. (His opinions were that everything cost too much.)

Here's the view from someone who can afford what she wants:

Well, first, Chanel is worth the money because everything they sell is top of the line quality. Handbags are generally classic in design, and they'll last 10–20 years, easy. The leather is a superior quality: get a scratch, just take a tissue and gently rub it out. The leather is soft enough to look flawless for years. As for the plated metals etc., Chanel's Boutique will refinish it for the life of the item. This is true not only of their handbags, but of shoes, jewelry, etc. (And speaking of jewelry, I own their $5,000 Deux Etoiles ring. Why was it worth $5,000? Because, first, it's based on an original 1932 Coco Chanel design which should indicate to you it's ultimate timelessness. Second, because of the quality of the diamonds which generally can't be matched by your typical jeweler ... unless you're looking at Tiffany's and Cartier, and still, you'd be hard pressed to walk out of there with a ring like this for anything less than $10,000.)

Clothing: Chanel's suits and dresses generally don't go out of style. They simply update – via minor tweaking – the same looks that Coco created in the 50s/60s, so again, the timelessness of these items is unquestionable. Once the tweak goes out of style, you're merely wearing rare Chanel vintage. I say go for it and do it with confidence!

Most importantly, the quality of fabric and stitching guarantees that the item will stand the test of time and wear. Even when no one can see the Chanel label anywhere on your dress/suit/jacket/ etc., you look like a million bucks for as long as you own the item.

Cosmetics: Chanel has the longest staying power (especially their nail polishes.) Colors can look both trendy and classic simultaneously. Packaging is solid and virtually unbreakable.

> Michael Kors: He's a genius of a designer who's able to create trends while not straying too far from the classics. Unlike, say, Galliano, Kors' clothes are actually wearable in everyday situations. And again, it comes down to quality, quality, quality.[46]

Putting aside the opinions of your own in-groups, then buying an unbranded bag for £20 which lasts a year is much better value than buying a famously luxurious one for £2000 which lasts 25 years. (Although if you already have enough money to last you 25 years, who's worried?) If we are able to ignore the intellectual property rights violation of buying a counterfeit from someone who is profiting from another's creativity, then buying a fake for £50 which lasts for a year is still better value than keeping the real thing for only 25 years. Ethics not withstanding, with counterfeit goods you may receive something that has value, possibly more practical value than the real branded item. Say you pay $10 for a counterfeit watch which lasts five years and the branded original is priced at $500. To get the same value in terms of useful service, it would have to last you for 250 years.

At the same market you could buy an unbranded watch, designed by the same team who copy the Guccis and the Diors, also for $10. That will last you five years too. Does the fake Gucci have the same value as the unbranded watch? It would depend on how much value you attach to the brand name, rather than the quality of the item itself. If you had never heard of Gucci there would be absolutely no reason to buy the counterfeit over the unknown brand.

How about buying cheap batteries from a man with a table outside the train station? When we discover that they last five minutes instead of five weeks are we angry with the manufacturers, or the sellers, or with ourselves for being duped? What about when our faux-designer sunglasses fall apart after a week? Only if we have allowed someone to convince us that they were a terrific bargain.

For each of us there is a line which divides the two big reasons we make purchases, maintenance and desire, and where we draw our line depends upon influences like our disposable income, the group we socialize with, our upbringing, our background, and all those facets which influence the rest of our behavior.

Maintenance purchases are the ones we resent spending our money on, like buying fuel for a car, light bulbs, ink cartridges for the PC printer, or washing-up liquid. When we make maintenance purchases we look for value. Retailers have managed to blur the divide, to make spending our money relatively enjoyable, by stocking chocolate at the same place as you fill up your car, or putting a café at the DIY shop, but all the same, surely no one can actually enjoy spending money on batteries; it is a real nuisance and a grudge purchase.

Desire purchases are something we can look forward to, something exciting. The triumph of marketing has been to make maintenance purchases seem like desire purchases, to make spending money a pleasure with corresponding rewards, not a chore. Shopping is no longer a maintenance activity; it satisfies some of our desires, at least temporarily, even if they have only been artificially created by manufacturers and the hard work of their marketing teams.

If you can find a bargain, the annoyance of having to make a maintenance purchase is reduced a little by the small triumph of getting better value. Counterfeit batteries temporarily give you this triumph – until you find out that they last five minutes or leak inside your camera and the man you bought them from has disappeared.

Finding a bargain amongst your desire purchases adds to the pleasure or minimizes some of the guilt you feel at having spent money on non-essentials. A counterfeit handbag seems like a fantastic bargain; there's the added secret pleasure of thinking that no one you meet will be able to tell the difference (which immediately vanishes through one of life's waiting trapdoors if someone does spot it as a fake).

Do desire purchases make us happy? That's another story. If someone asks you, "Did it make you happy to snap up that pair of Gucci shoes in Milan at less than half the price you would normally pay in London?" do you say, "No, not after the first few hours. Shoes could never relieve me of the feeling of inner desolation which haunts me, knowing that I spend my life making money for directors and shareholders of a company which pollutes the atmosphere, underpays its workers, and leaves me no time to spend with my family, however, they [the shoes] temporarily assuage the misery and give me a feeling of mild glory when I detect the reluctant admiration of my co-workers," or do you say, "Absolutely! They are so beautiful and such a bargain!"

27
Brand damage: counterfeiters or customers?

In his book *Ancient Wisdom, Modern World: Ethics for the new millennium*, the Dalai Lama tells a tale about what happened when he found out his most senior and trusted advisers had gone behind his back and opened negotiations with the Chinese government. When China had occupied Tibet and banned Buddhism, the Dalai Lama, as the country's spiritual leader, had faced imprisonment or exile. Many of his fellow monks had been imprisoned and tortured so he had eventually chosen to leave to set up an alternative, temporary base in India from which to lead his exiled followers and campaign for China to leave his country. To discover that his closest friends and colleagues had taken this action was deeply hurtful to him. However, instead of blaming them he asked them what had he done to make them behave in this way. They told him that they were very sorry and they had considered this deeply, but as he was incapable of keeping a secret, they thought it better to do it without him. He considered this and decided that although he was still very disappointed in them, they were right; he would have found it impossible to keep the secret negotiations secret.

It is a regularly repeated view amongst luxury brands that counterfeits damage their brand identity, but the reality is by no means that simple. The Tommy Hilfiger brand was damaged, in the opinion of their management, by one of the customer groups that adopted the original Hilfiger upmarket identity and adapted it to their own.

And so to Burberry, whose recognizable checked design has been copied by all and sundry, and the tale of Daniella Westbrook, actor and former soap star, famous for being famous, for her successful rehabilitation following years of cocaine use, and for reconstructive surgery on her nose. (She visited the Lush shop in Brighton once, picked up a Bath Ballistic to smell the fragrance and got white powder on the end of her nose. No one dared tell her.)

Our Daniella bounced back from her abuse years. In 2004 she was pictured in a paparazzo shot, picking her baby out of its pushchair. So far, so usual. The thing was that the baby was wearing a Burberry checked kilt; the pushchair was covered in the same fabric; Daniella herself was wearing a matching Burberry kilt with a checked Burberry bag to match. The photograph was widely circulated in the gossip and fashion magazines; in *B* magazine in March 2005 it was included in the "trendstopper" section.

Was this the turning point in the check's rise and rise, which dated back to Rose Marie Bravo's appointment in 1997, or merely a localized blip? As a New Yorker, Rose Marie Bravo was rather a surprise appointment for Burberry's, the raincoat manufacturer established in 1856, which had been declining with dignity in a particularly British way since around 1955 when it was bought by GUS. In 1950, when my mother saved up her first wages and bought a Burberry mac, it was the height of chic. (The tale of her wearing it around the Middlesbrough council estate where she lived with her mother is part of the Bain/McCartney family heritage; she was tutted at for acting above her station by disapproving matrons of respectable working-class families.) The check was only found on the inside although in the 1980s yuppies would leave their coats unbuttoned so that the lining could flap happily in the breeze for all to see. People recognized it; it was one of those brand symbols which pulled all the right strings and made the symbolic values pop into your head at first sight.

Burberry bounced back and became fashionable once again when Bravo brought in Gucci designer Christopher Bailey to rejuvenate it. In the *Guardian* René Carayol wrote:

> Turnover has doubled, profits have soared and she has diversified into many different areas. Bravo has said that the famous picture of supermodel Kate Moss in a Burberry check bra cut the average age of Burberry's customers by some 30 years.

Umbrellas, luggage, and scarves had been around since 1967; that was a pretty natural brand extension for a waterproof mac company but it was the point at which the check started to take over the brand. When the flagship store opened in Bond Street in 2000 there were clothes, shoes, boots, bags of all shapes and sizes. The place was plastered with checks.

Now there is – no prizes for guessing – a perfume: Burberry Brit, launched just about the time that the whole Brit thing was becoming a bit tired in Britain.

Where Kate Moss goes, the pack follows; in 2005 if Kate carries a bag, the bag becomes big; she wears a belt, it appears in every clothes shop in the United Kingdom; she made Ugg boots a big, international brand where previously they had been a small Australian one. I wonder if it annoys her at all to see the entire world copying her every move or if she enjoys it. Recently she stated that the waistcoat was her favorite item of clothing; perhaps she did it as a little joke to see if she could get the world to wear them.

Burberry's appeal then spread from middle to the wealthier working classes, the British boys and girls who love to flash their cash, have a laugh, go out, get smashed, and don't care what anyone thinks about it. A group emerged, the "chavs." In the 1940s they might have been "spivs" (the opposite of VIPs). The previous generation was known as Kevins and Sharons because they stuck their names at the top of their Ford Escort dashboards. The best explanation I've heard for the source of the word "chav" is that it is derived from "Cheltenham Average." Cheltenham Ladies College is an exclusive private boarding school for girls. Rumor has it that Cheltenham Ladies were the ones who attended the school and Cheltenham Averages were the ones around town who didn't. They were labeled chavs and so it spread – possibly. My grandmother would probably have called them "common as muck" but this has never been an indication of spending power; look at Napoleon, a prime example of how wealth can't buy taste. Chavs with less cash would buy counterfeit Burberry, of which there was suddenly a lot around; it increased in proportion to the amount of publicity that real Burberry generated.

Chavs wanted the stuff with the checks on; the media picked up on this and the people who had previously bought Burberry because of the checks dropped it like a stone. In the National Theatre's sell-out production of *His Dark Materials*, a young mother was pictured walking around Oxford's botanical gardens; the audience knew that we were watching a scene from our own world, not the parallel universes the characters had been visiting, because the girl was wearing a chav track suit and pushing a Burberry check stroller.

Customers who chose the brand for the styling, cut, and quality had plenty of reasons to continue buying, but the check's appeal faded so badly that Burberry' sales fell for the first time during Bravo's reign at the beginning of 2005.

Counterfeit Burberry bags are available on every street stall, scarves with the check – or a design so similar that the average person can't tell the difference – sell wherever you can find scarves. Every luggage shop sells a range of suitcases on wheels with the check on them. Of the very few copies I saw in Japan, the most obvious was a beige scarf with a black, red, and white check on it. Even the law-abiding Japanese had succumbed to temptation.

Of course Burberry will recover; they do not rely on their check; they used it as a springboard to send them vaulting out of the doldrums back into the world of luxury brands. The products, the real ones, are well designed and made from good quality materials, and will last the course; much of it is beautiful, luxury stuff, with scarcely a check in sight.

Should they throw up their hands in horror and blame the chavs for cheapening their brand? Or should they ask the chavs what made them want to buy it? Perhaps they should be asking Daniella Westbrook who wore only the real thing and was accused of cheapening the brand.

Do counterfeits steal sales from genuine brands? It is a question of scale and timing. Many people who would buy branded batteries for £3 would also buy fakes for £1.50, particularly those who are naturally trusting and believe the vendors' lies. People who want a genuine Chanel bag at $800 are unlikely ever to buy a fake – within a certain timescale. Those who start out buying fakes when they are young can trade up as they grow older and better off. In our research, those who admitted to having bought them said things like "it was in the past when I was young and didn't know any better" and those who thought it was acceptable tended to be young. For luxury brands, counterfeits could be considered to be free advertising, if their brand guardians were feeling particularly magnanimous about it. From the tobacco, electronic media, and alcohol brands, counterfeits do steal sales. The dangers, both personal and on a wider scale, are outweighed by the appeal of an apparent bargain.

Where does the Dalai Lama fit into this? He recommends that when we feel that the world has been unjust to us, we should look around us to see what we might have done to cause this to happen. That's not to say that we should accept the blame for everything that ever goes wrong, just that if we accept responsibility for our share of it, then we may be better prepared to prevent it happening again. Advertising phenomenally expensive brands with considerable mark-ups, creating a desire amongst people who can't afford them, accepting the profits from the massive expansion that has been the good fortune of many luxury brands since the 1980s, then expecting individuals not to reflect the same "I want it and I want it now" view that businesses have shown – that is a trifle unrealistic.

A letter arrived at my place last week addressed to my husband; I confiscated it. The envelope said:

Why shouldn't your life meet your expectations?

Inside it said:

> Your life needs new floors, a motorbike and an African safari. The new American Express® Platinum Credit Card says, 'Why not?'

Why not? Because a public servant on an average wage can't currently afford new floors, a motorbike, and an African safari even on a typical 8.9 percent variable APR.

We are calmed, soothed, and encouraged in the West into believing that we can have all we want whenever we want it; superficially that gives a much warmer glow than to deny ourselves until we've saved up. If chavs see Burberry and chavs like it, then isn't their money as good as anyone else's? If it's fake, so what? It's still got the check on it that Kate Moss had on her bra and knickers. When a brand's symbolic values have been hyped until they outstrip the functional attributes, there's no telling what will happen to it, but you can bet it won't all be good.

When a brand's guardians want to know if they are about to be copied, all they have to do is look at eBay. If their brand is selling second-hand for significant sums, then the symbolic values have captured the market's collective attention; it's ripe for a rip-off.

28
Is it serious?

Does it matter whether or not we buy counterfeits?

Making a fashion item that is inspired by another designer's work is just the way it goes in the fashion business.

Deliberately copying someone else's work in the fashion industry and making it up in cheaper materials is accepted. An observer from outside the fashion business may consider it to be morally wrong, but most are probably happy to buy something trendy which they can afford, oblivious as to whether it has been copied or not.

Doing either of the above in a different industry infringes intellectual property law and criminal or civil action could be taken against the copycats.

All the above generally take place between organizations which operate above the law and pay their taxes, and it does not fund any criminal activities (apart from the accountants' and designers' occasional (alleged) use of recreational drugs).

Buying a copy of a garment or an accessory is not illegal, nor is it aiding and abetting criminals or depriving our governments of revenue which they spend on running our countries. The designer may be annoyed or flattered at the speed at which his or her influential work is imitated.

Manufacturing counterfeit goods in a country where the IP law is not applied in the same way as the West is not considered to be wrong within that country. Those manufacturers are operating within their own laws and financial systems (like Señor Pelletier and his Cartiers in Mexico).

If you were a Chinese business man with a bag factory and you discovered that if you made exactly the same bag as before but with a logo all over it, people would pay ten times more for it than they did the plain one, what would you do?

Would you also sell them to people who offered you cash, no questions asked?

Buying a single counterfeit bag, a watch and a t-shirt from a manufacturer or retailer overseas and bringing them back to the United States with you for your own use is legal as long as you don't do it more than once every 30 days. It encourages the Chinese to break intellectual property laws and probably irritates the luxury brand owners no end, and it may make the purchasers feel a twang of guilt for pretending to be people they are not (people who can afford the real thing), but it does not fund organized crime or endanger anyone's life or health, so it could be worse.

Buying the same stuff and taking it back to France lands you in much hotter water.

Buying a counterfeit piece of clothing or a fashion accessory from an Internet source does not necessarily fund organized crime. It may have come from a Chinese manufacturer via a small business or a student in Hong Kong. They are probably not paying their taxes on it, but they are unlikely to be involved in prostitution, people trafficking, gun running, terrorism, or drug smuggling. The result is probably cheap goods and a feeling of disappointment for purchasers, but as the quality of counterfeits is improving, the buyers might be happy with the purchase.

The designs' owners may claim that they have lost profit, but as someone who was buying a fake would be unlikely to pay ten times as much for a real one, in reality their sales are unlikely to be damaged. Perhaps, like the upper classes and their jewels, those who can afford them like to buy both but only take out the fakes in public to avoid their being damaged or stolen.

A counterfeit piece of clothing or an accessory bought in Europe or the United States was imported or manufactured illegally and in quantity, probably by an organized crime set-up. Profits from the sale are generally untaxed, so government revenue is lost, and earnings could be funding more dangerous crime. There are anomalies like shops in London's Covent Garden opening selling counterfeit fashion products, charging VAT, and paying their taxes. They are breaking intellectual property law but their retail business is legitimate.

Luxury brands' images might be devalued by the sight of average people walking around wearing their logos. This is what the luxury brands' guardians claim; however in the case of Burberry it was the sight of famous people walking around in the real thing which did the most damage, so the jury is out on that one. Some people consider that using the wrong celebrity in their advertisements or having their bags carried by tens of thousands of Japanese office workers does a brand more damage than counterfeits do.

Safety-critical fakes are despicable. Whether their manufacturers are legitimate companies or operated by criminals, the results are inexcusable.

One widely held view is that all cigarette manufacture is despicable, legal or not; however, we now know that cigarettes cause many illnesses and this is marked on the packets. Those who buy them are aware of this, even though they choose to believe that it will never happen to them or use the statistically unsound excuse that they could be run over by a bus. (They could, but that merely adds to their risk of an early death; it doesn't replace it.)

To supply something labeled as vodka, but which is lethally poisonous after one glass, is murder. In the United Kingdom in 2003 a death was known to be caused by counterfeit vodka. Deaths are also caused by drinking genuine vodka but the drinker is aware of the dangers. Selling "perfume" which contains urine, "medicines" with no active ingredient, poison labeled as olive oil, or caustic soda in washing powder boxes is a criminal act, incomprehensible to anyone with a shred of decency.

As long as there are people trying to make a quick buck and others trying to save one, inadequate resources to prevent this and a general view that it's not such a terrible thing to steal a trademark from an established brand, the trade in counterfeits will flourish. In the West we have a choice; we can buy at supermarkets and corner shops or we can have a go at grabbing a bargain at car boot (trunk) sales, or from some bloke at the pub. It's where the choice doesn't exist that the law needs to extend its long arm.

Is it a genuinely serious problem, or are governments just spinning the organized crime aspects of counterfeiting in order to scare people into paying their sales taxes?

The UK's National Criminal Intelligence Service's criteria for defining organized crime are:[47]

> Mandatory criteria:
>   Collaboration between at least three persons.
>   Prolonged criminal activity.
>   Commission of serious crimes.
>   Crimes motivated by power or profit.
> Secondary criteria:
>   International, national or regional operations
>   Use of violence, intimidation or corruption.
>   Use of commercial structures.
>   Money laundering.
>   Influencing politicians, public authorities, the
>   media, judges, etc.

For those of us who have no connections with the criminal underground, don't have any experience of its operations, and imagine that it can't really be all that bad, the NCIS website is fascinating reading. I strongly recommend that you visit. In their 2002 report on the scale of organized crime, there was no mention of IP crime, but the 2003 report said this:

> Intellectual property crime is taking place on a vast scale globally. Advances in technology have facilitated its growth, by enabling the speedy reproduction of high quality counterfeit goods, the best of which are difficult to differentiate from the genuine

articles. The counterfeiting of CDs, DVDs and other digital media, much of it done in the Far East, is well-publicised, but the counterfeiting of all types of goods from designer clothes to pharmaceuticals is also rife. Many serious and organised criminals are involved, either in the manufacture of counterfeit products, or in their distribution, attracted by the high profits and the low risk of detection, and no doubt conscious of the fact that the penalties for intellectual property crime offences are rarely more than minimal. Meanwhile, there remains a public perception of intellectual property crime as a victimless crime, despite the fact that certain counterfeit products, such as car or aircraft parts, pharmaceuticals and alcohol, pose a direct risk to the public. Where serious and organised criminals are involved, it is reasonable to assume that a proportion of the profits is used to fund other serious crimes.[48]

In 2002 a reader might have concluded that counterfeiting didn't present a serious problem; within a year it had earned its own subsection. This is not a cover for a revenue issue; it is a real problem, but awareness of it is low. People buy counterfeits because they currently can't see any good reason not to. Smokers know that cigarettes could kill them but they still smoke. In the same spirit, counterfeits may be linked to terrorism but if you buy one, the bomb probably wouldn't actually land on you, personally. It's a question of scale. Wherever there are serious quantities of counterfeit products being moved around the globe, that's where the serious, illegal gains are being made. Please be assured that there is more trade in illegal counterfeits than most of us could possibly envisage.

One widely held view is that luxury brands charge too much and deserve to be copied, but – and for the last time –

as grandma would have said, "Two wrongs don't make a right." Someone who justifies buying a counterfeit by claiming that the luxury brands' profits are too high has been attracted by that brand's own publicity, and the best way to lower their profits is to buy something legal but completely different. Feeling a temptation to buy a fake Gucci from eBay (if eBay don't spot it first), a faux Louis Vuitton from a Venice street trader, or an authentic counterfeit Prada from a smart Sri Lankan boutique is admitting that our desire for it has overtaken our common sense. A counterfeit's manufacturers have stolen someone else's design and theft is wrong, no matter how trivial it may appear in comparison with faking medicines and baby milk. Buying their product might only serve as more advertising for the luxury brand, which would be contrary to the anti-brand campaigner's intentions. Then again, a $795 bag for $30 is enough to tempt the most moral of bargain hunters. Who am I to judge, having failed at the final hurdle and smuggled my authentic counterfeit Alma back into the United Kingdom?

Currently fortune favors the faker. The law can't catch up with counterfeiters; neither the intellectual property lawyers nor the enforcement officers are able to stop counterfeiters who are making and selling cheap and sometimes dangerous copies of branded goods. Where we are fortunate enough to have the choice, the power is in the hands and pockets of the consumer. In the billion dollar market for counterfeit branded clothes and accessories, we can vote with our wallets.

I would advise everyone to avoid anything you can smoke, swallow, or put on your body if it could be from an unreliable source. I would never risk putting a battery bought from a street trader into a piece of valuable electrical equipment. These things are not bargains.

As for the fashion business, I would recommend taking more time to decide who is pushing your brand buttons and pulling your shopping strings. Our own latent talents are being suppressed by the lack of time we have in our lives for our own ideas to blossom and our creative skills to be tested. Brands offer instant coolness; all we have to do is buy them. Goodness gracious, but there are some beautiful things to buy out there! But the more we buy, the more we must earn and the less time we have to think for ourselves. Counterfeits can offer instant coolness at a bargain price, but at the expense of stealing ideas that belong to others. Anyway, is being cool such a marvelous thing?

There are two ways in which human beings learn, experimentation and copying; most advances in thought and action are a combination of the two, taking what we've already learned elsewhere and trying something slightly different to see what happens. Let's take some time to dream up some ideas of our own. There are more than enough people ready to steal others' ideas. Let's cut the strings, give ourselves the space to think, and fill the world with more creativity, preferably our own.

NOTES

1   www.customs.gov

2   www.itnarchive.com

3   www.itnarchive.com

4   Sally Vincent, "How I did it," *Guardian*, October 23, 2004.

5   G. Hankinson and P. Cowking, *Branding in Action*, McGraw-Hill, 1993.

6   W. G. Nickels and M. B. Wood, *Marketing: Relationships, Quality, Value,* Worth Publishers, 1997.

7   www.poolonline.com/archive/iss6fea5.htlm

8   G. Williams, *Branded? Products and their personalities*, V&A Publications, 2000.

9   *Financial Times* How to spend it, February 2005.

10   www.newfaces.com

11   *Sydney Morning Herald*, www.smh.com.au, January 25, 2005.

12   As above.

13   Cass Creatives Report: *So Logo! Branding in the 21st century*, Cass Business School, October 13, 2004.

14   Our own research, 2004.

15   Nicholas Redfearn, Rouse & Co. International, www.iprights.com, August 2004.

16   C. Classen and D. Howes, 'The dynamics and ethics of cross-cultural consumption', in D. Howes (ed.) *Cross-Cultural Consumption*, Routledge, 1996.

17   Jonathan Fenby, *Piracy and the Public: Forgery, theft and exploitation*, Muller, 1983.

18   As above.

19   Around 1994: I was there at the time.

20   *Marketing Week*, April 28, 2005.

21   Our own research, 2004.

22   *Observer*, April 17, 2005.

23   A Customs guide for travellers entering the UK, http://customs.hmrc.gov.uk

24   www.info-france-usa.org
25   As above.
26   www.cepsghana.org/gov_corp.cfm?GovCorpID=8
27   www.rcs.co.id/kepabean_10_1995_eng.htm
28   www.customs.govt.nz/importers/Prohibited+Imports/
      default.htm
29   This adds up to 97 percent. We don't know what the US
      government did with the other 3 percent: rounded the
      figures down perhaps? Anyway it's not our fault the
      figures are wrong.
30   http://www.customs.gov/xp/cgov/travel/vacation/kbyg/
      prohibited_restricted.xml#
      TrademarkedandCopyrightedArticles
31   Personal conversation, 2005.
32   www.teentoday.co.uk
33   Our own research, 2004.
34   www.pensionscommission.org.uk/publications/2004/
      annrep/fullreport.pdf
35   www.which.net
36   Eric Hobsbawm, *The Age of Extremities*, Abacus, 1994.
37   Russell Ash, Marissa Piesman and Marilee Hartley, *The
      Official British Yuppie Handbook*, Ravette, 1984.
38   *Financial Times* How to spend it, October 2004.
39   'When imposters knock off profits,'
      www.brandchannel.com, December 11, 2003.
40   Simon Garfield, *Mauve: How one man invented a colour
      that changed the world*, Faber & Faber, 2000.
41   Stuart Sutherland, *Irrationality: The enemy within*,
      Penguin, 1994.
42   Personal conversation with Nike UK marketing director.
43   *New*, Issue 096, UK.
44   *Eve*, March 2005.
45   *Eve*, November 2004.
46   Our own research, 2004.
47   www.ncis.co.uk
48   www.ncis.co.uk/ukta/2003/threat01.asp

BIBLIOGRAPHY

Ash, Russell, Hartley, Marilee and Piesman, Marissa (1984) *The Official British Yuppie Handbook*. Ravette.

Barthes, Roland (1957) *Mythologies*. Vintage (2000 edn).

de Botton, Alain (2004) *Status Anxiety*. Penguin (2005 edn).

Boyle, David (2003) *Authenticity: Brands, Fakes, Spin and the Lust for Real Life*. Harper Perennial (2004 edn).

Bstan-'dzin-rgya-mtsho, Dalai Lama XIV (2001) *Ancient Wisdom, Modern World: Ethics for the new millennium*. Abacus.

Bullmore, Jeremy (2003) *More Bullmore Behind the Scenes in Advertising (Mark III)*. World Advertising Research Centre.

Dariaux, Genevieve Antoine (2004) *A Guide to Elegance*. Harper Collins.

Davis, Jennifer (2003) *Intellectual Property Law*. Butterworths.

Fellowes, Julian (2004) *Snobs*. QPD.

Finlay, Victoria (2002) *Colour*. Sceptre.

Garfield, Simon (2000) *Mauve: How one man invented a colour that changed the world*, Faber & Faber.

Hankinson, Graham and Cowking, Phillippa (1993) *Branding in Action*. McGraw-Hill.

Hart, Susannah and Murphy, John (eds) (1998) *Brands: The new wealth creators*. Palgrave.

Hobsbawm, Eric (1962) *The Age of Revolution 1789–1848*. Cardinal (1988 edn).

Hobsbawm, Eric (1975) *The Age of Capital 1848–1875*. Cardinal (1988 edn).

Hobsbawm, Eric (1987) *The Age of Empire 1875–1914*. Abacus (2003 edn).

Hobsbawm, Eric (1994) *The Age of Extremes 1914–1994*. Abacus (1995 edn).

Hodgkinson, Tom (2005) *How to be Idle*. Harper Collins.

Johnson, Anna (2002) *Handbags: The power of the purse*. Workman.

Lewis, David and Bridger, Darren (2000) *The Soul of the New Consumer*. Nicholas Brealey (2004 edn).

Orwell, George (1946) *Why I Write*. Penguin (2004 edn).

Packard, Vance (1959) *The Status Seekers*. Penguin (1966 edn).

Pinker, Stephen (1997) *How the Mind Works*. Norton.

Pooler, Jim (2003) *Why We Shop: Emotional rewards and retail strategies*. Praeger.

Quart, Alissa (2003) *Branded™: The buying and selling of teenagers*. Arrow.

Rogers, Everett (1962) *Diffusion of Innovations*. Free Press.

Sivananda (1964) *Bliss Divine*. Sivananda Press (1967 edn).

Smiles, Samuel (1859) *Self-Help*. John Murray (1876 edn).

Sutherland, Stuart (1992) *Irrationality: The enemy within*. Penguin (1994 edn).

Thackeray, William (1848) *Vanity Fair*. Oxford University Press (1983 edn).

Trollope, Anthony (1873) *The Way We Live Now*. Oxford University Press (1992 edn).

Various (1998) *The Fashion Book*. Phaidon (2004 edn).

Wharton, Edith (1937) *The Buccaneers*. Fourth Estate (1994 edn).

Williams, Gareth (2000) *Branded? Products and their personalities*. V&A.

INDEX

Absolutely Fabulous 182
Adidas 4, 18, 113
Aero 21, 78
Ageh, Tony 152
Aguilera, Christina 186
Alessi 135
Allah 67
American Express 211
American National Book Award 169
Anhui province 5
Ansoff, Igor 78–80
Antik Batik 117
Aqua di Parma 106
Arcadia Group 13
Arden, Elizabeth 4, 185
Armani 4, 158
Arnault, Bernard 31–2, 98, 161
Asda 21, 186
Au Printemps 158
Audi 134
Australia 146

Baby Phat 69, 178
Bailey, Christopher 207
Bain, Elizabeth 126
Barnes, Julian 190
Batista government 11
BBC 20, 23–4, 55
Beatles, The 20
Beckham, David 21
Belgium 4
Benefit 106
Bensoussan, Robert 114
Berlin 144
Berne Convention for the Protection of
     Literary and Artistic Works (1886)
     150
Berry, Halle 185
Beyoncé 162
Bhs 13

"Black Wednesday" 129
Blanchett, Cate 162
Bliss 186
Bloomingdale's 90, 113
Blue Dal 190
BMW 138
Boden 114
Body Shop 21, 42
Bond Street 30, 42, 208
Boots 42, 158
Bradman, Don 4
Brando, Marlon 22
Bravo, Rose Marie 207, 209
Bridgwater, Duke of 171
Brighton 206
Brindley, James 171
British Airways 61
Buddha 126
Buddhism 206
"Bugger-all-money" 139
Burberry 4, 8, 20, 38, 55, 69, 72, 82,
     95, 113, 131, 136, 163, 178,
     206–11, 216
Burk Wood, Marian 27
Burton 13
Butterfly 159–62

Cacharel 21, 159
Cadbury 20, 78
Caesar, Julius 20
Campari 28
Canada 11, 87
Canal Street 35, 46, 91, 92
Canon 4, 61
Cape Town 83
Carayol, René 207
Cardin, Pierre 158
Cartier 4, 51, 53, 85, 91, 142, 200,
     214
Casablanca 110

Castro, Fidel 11
Chambre Syndicale de la Haute
   Couture 158
Chanel 8, 15, 32, 34, 40, 46, 56, 95,
   100–2, 158–9, 191, 200, 210
Charbonnel et Walker 21
Charles, Prince of Wales 115
Chase, Lorraine 28
Chaumet 106
Cheltenham Ladies College 208
China 4–6, 33, 56, 87, 92, 154, 206
Chloé 186
Choo, Jimmy 18, 114
Chopard 4, 91, 92
CIA 50, 153
Citroen 19
Claire's Accessories 18
Clarks Shoes 115
Clifton, Rita 39, 80
Coffee Republic 64
Cohiba Cuban cigars 11
Colombia 127
Conran, Jasper 159–61
Constantine, Mark 94, 146–7, 149
Copenhagen 7
Costa Coffee 64
Covent Garden 95, 191, 215
Cowking, Philippa 19, 28
Crisp, Quentin 68
Cruise, Tom 20
Cuba 10–11
Custo Barcelona 114
Customs 86–8

Dalai Lama 206, 210
Dallas 192
Debenhams 159, 160
Denmark 7
Dents 177
Design Museum 191
di Gregorio, Marco 177
Diana, Princess of Wales 115
Dior, Christian 4, 32, 34, 55, 71, 82,
   89–92, 95, 103, 106, 111, 154, 158
DKNY 158
Doc Martens 110
Dolce & Gabbana 18
Dominican Republic 11
Doncaster 4

Dorothy Perkins 13
Douglas, Michael 127
Dresser, Christopher 95
Dubai 82
Duracell 4
Dutch, Von 4, 34–6, 69, 91
Dyson 114

eBay 80, 96–106, 111, 117, 211, 219
Elizabeth II, Queen 20
Elle 186
eLuxury.com 90, 104, 106
Enfield, Harry 139
Etam 13, 186
Eugenie, Empress 162
Europe 6, 90, 112–17, 122, 154, 215
Eve 61, 184
Evisu 18
"Eye Love" designs 98, 102, 105

Farthingale 166
FCUK 71
Fellowes, Julian 135–6
Fenby, Jonathan 54
Fendi 4, 55, 106, 178, 192
Ferretti, Alberta 185
Financial Times 32, 160, 161
Flett, Kathryn 82
Foot, Michael 135
Ford 20, 138–9, 208
France 53, 89, 111, 162, 215
Franks, Lynn 182
Friedman, Vanessa 137

Gainsborough, Thomas 136
Galliano 71, 201
Gap, The 20–1, 70
Garfield, Simon 163
Garrard 18
Gateshead 139, 190
Gaultier, Jean-Paul 158–60
Gehring, Fred 114–16
Gekko, Gordon 127
Givenchy 4, 32, 34, 106, 178
Glasgow 139
Google 80, 100, 102, 127
Greece 4
Green & Black's 21, 61, 80
Green, Philip 13, 154

Guardian 13, 152, 207
Gucci 4, ,46, 55–6, 70, 82–4, 92, 95,
    103, 111, 120, 134, 146, 154, 201,
    203, 207, 219
Guerlain 4, 106
GUS 207

Hammersmith College 31
Hankinson, Professor Graham 19, 21,
    22, 28
Harley-Davidson 33–4
Harrods 130
Harvard Business Review 61, 143,
    165
Hasselblad 123
Havana 10
Hayward Gallery 190
HBO 192
Heathrow Airport 42
Hello! 183
Hennessey 106
Hermès 4, 51, 54, 56, 85, 186
Highland Spring water 42
Hilfiger, Tommy 82, 114–16, 206
Hirohito, Emperor 54
His Dark Materials 209
Hitler, Adolf 35, 67
Hobsbawm, Eric 122
Hodgkinson, Tom 171
Hollywood 127
Honda 33
Hong Kong 13, 56, 84, 85, 87, 163,
    193, 215
Howard, Kenneth 34–5
HSBC 20
Hudson, Kate 162
Hush Puppy 38–9

India 4, 95, 206
Indonesia 5, 86
intellectual property 146–55
Interbrand 26, 39, 80
Internet 23, 41, 64, 74, 90, 99, 187,
    191, 215
Interpol 5, 50
Intourist 10
Ireland 6
Isetan 113
Italy 6, 51, 64, 146, 171

ITN 6
ITV News 3

Jackson, Michael 21
Jacobs, Marc 67, 98, 106, 159
James, Henry 130
Japan 54–6, 78, 98, 105, 146,
    209
JLo *see* Lopez, Jennifer
Johansson, Scarlett 162
Jolie, Angelina 186

Karan, Donna 106, 159
KDV 113
Kenya 6
Kenzo 106, 110
Kishimoto, Eley 185
KitKat 38, 78
Klein, Calvin 84
Knightsbridge 163
Korea 56
Kors, Michael 186, 201
Kosinski, Jerzi 169
Kotsu Times 56
Kroll, Tanner 114
Krug 106
Kuala Lumpur 84, 89, 120

La Redoute 159, 160
La Rochefoucauld, Francois 184
Labour Party 135
Lacoste 4, 70, 134
Lacroix 158
Lagerfeld, Karl 159
Lamont, Norman 129
Lang, Helmut 161
Laughing Cow cheese 4
Lauren, Ralph 4, 8, 116, 153
Lavigne, Avril 162
Le Bon Marché 106, 113
Lea & Perrins 4
Leeds 4
Levis 4, 54
Levitt, Theodore 165
Life of Brian 180
Liverpool 139
Livingstone, Ken 183
"Loadsamoney" 139
Locke, John 13, 149–50

Lomo 61
London 7, 20, 24, 39, 64, 74, 98,
 126, 190–1
 mayoral election 183
 School of Fashion 169
 shopping 8, 30, 38, 42, 95, 179,
  203, 215
 Transport Museum 191
Lopez, Jennifer 21, 69, 178–80
Lui, Judy 3, 18, 112
Lur Saluces, Compte Alexandre 31–2
Lush 61, 65–6, 80, 94, 146–8, 206
Lush Times 147
LVMH (Louis Vuitton Moët Hennessy)
 31, 71, 90, 98, 104, 106, 161
Lyon 163

M&Ms 190
Madonna 21
Madrid Agreements 151
Malaysia 84
Malle, Frederic 21
Manchester 139
Manchester United 4
Mandarina Duck 176, 177
Marie Claire 185–6
Marrakech 4, 111, 153, 179
Mars 22, 78–80
Mauritius 153
McCartney, Sarah 106
Mercedes 123, 138
Mexico 53, 214
Mexico City 53
Miami 42
Middlesbrough 95, 207
Milan 11, 55, 203
Milky Way 79
Mills, Mandy 35
Ming dynasty 191
Miss Moneypenny 161
Miss Pinky 55
Miss Selfridge 13
Missoni 186
Miu Miu 185
Mizrahi, Isaac 38
Moët et Chandon 106
Moisannite 4
Monsoon 18
Mont Blanc 30

Monte Carlo 115
Montevideo 4, 154
Monty Python 180
Morocco 110, 111
Moschino 71
Moss, Kate 186, 207–8, 211
Mr Muscle 31
Muji 80
Mumm Cordon Rouge champagne 4
Murakami, Takashi 67, 90, 92, 94,
 98, 105, 106, 111
Musée de la Contrefaçon 2–3, 42, 113
Museum of Modern Art (MoMA)
 190–1
Mykonos 82

Napoleon I (Bonaparte) 20, 209
Napoleon III 162
National Criminal Intelligence Service
 (NCIS) 217
National Theatre 209
Nelson, Prince Rogers 74
Nestlé 78
New 184
New York 35, 38, 46, 84, 90, 92, 96,
 190, 192, 207
New Zealand 84, 86
Newcastle 117, 139
Nickels, William 27
Nike 4, 74, 116, 170, 195
Nikon 123
Northern Ireland 6
Now 185

O'Brien, Diane 154
Oakley 4, 84
Observer 61
Olympic Games 4, 170
Olympus 20, 123
Oscar 127
Oxford Street 8, 64
Oxford University 31

Pacella, Marietta 68, 96, 111
Pakistan 4
Paperchase 61
Paris 2, 11, 84,
 and brand identity 20
 shopping 13–14, 66, 76, 112, 177

style 55
Paris Convention for the Protection of Intellectual Property (1883) 150
Parker, Sarah Jessica 162
Partagas 10
Pasquet, Eve 146
Patent Convention Treaty 151
Pelletier, Fernando 53, 214
Penguin Books 31
Pentagon 5
Pepsi 21
Perkin, William 162, 163
Perrier 4, 42, 43
Peugeot 138
Philippines 5
Pink, Thomas 106
piracy, of products 5, 8, 60, 85–6
Pooler, Professor Jim 192–3
Porsche 22, 130, 134, 137, 138, 194
Potter, Harry 4
Prada 41, 55, 71, 83, 154, 161, 219
"Preppie" 134
Price, Linda 169
Primark 71, 186
Prince see Nelson, Prince Rogers
Pucci 106
Pumas 170
Purdey 134

Qantas 20

Radley 21, 74
Readers' Digest 60
Reagan, Ronald 120, 127–8, 137, 193
Red 186
Red Bull 80
Red, Ecko 69
Renault 4, 138
Rentokil 31
Revlon 20
Rocha, John 159–60
Rogers, Everett 164–5
Rolex 50
Rolls-Royce 130
Rothwell, Caroline 34
Rouse & Co. International 52
Rowntree 78
Russia 6
Sag Harbor 70

Sainsbury 161
Saint Laurent, Yves (YSL) 32, 34, 158
Samaritaine 106
Savile Row 1444
Seattle 38
Second World War 122
Selfridges 113
Sex and the City 192
Simmons, Kimora Lee 178
Singapore 6
"Sloane" 134
Smarties 190
Smith, Adam 128
Smurfs 4
Smythson 61
Snickers 79
Sony 20, 116
Spade, Kate 4, 42, 91
Spain 82, 111, 122
Spears, Britney 35
Springspotter Network 172
Star Wars 20
Starbucks 20, 38, 64, 65, 80
Stevens, Rachel 184
Strok, Gharani 159
Sutherland, Stuart 165
Swatch 91, 182
Sweden 66
Switzerland 87
Sydney 38

TAG Heuer 106
Taipei 83
Taiwan 56, 83, 87, 146
Tanner Krolle 21, 114
Tate Modern 39–40
Tatler 185
Teen Today web forum 102, 104
Tenerife 84
Tesco 115, 116, 161
Tetley 4
Thailand 85
Thatcher, Margaret 120, 127–8, 137, 142, 193
The Bay 113
Tibet 206
Tiffany 18, 200
Timberland 4, 113–14
TKMaxx 114–17, 176, 177

Tokyo 54, 55, 97
Topman 13
Topshop 13, 18, 117
Tupperware 42
"Turbo Nutter Bastard" 139
Turkey 82
Turkish Delight 78
Twix 79

Ugg 198, 208
Unilever 66–7
Union des Fabricants 3, 50, 150
United Kingdom 20, 72, 80, 110,
    195
  companies 13, 28, 115, 148, 159,
    171
  and fakes 3, 187, 216, 219
  financial culture 120–2, 128–30,
    135–6, 139
  law 7, 11, 89
  shopping 82, 208
United Nations 151
United States 171
  companies 65–6, 115
  and fakes 6, 41
  financial culture 120–2, 126–7,
    130
  law 11, 88–9, 154–5, 214–15
US Customs and Border Protection
    department 3

V&A Museum 191
Van Gogh, Vincent 4
van Noten, Dries 185
van Wyck, Henry 60
Venice 51, 219

Versace 18, 69–70, 113, 185
Victoria, Queen 162, 163
Vietnam 5, 84
Vogue 186
Volkswagen (VW) 74, 123, 138
Vuitton, Louis 3–4, 18, 21, 31, 51,
    54–6, 67, 69–70, 82, 90–2, 94–106,
    110–14, 154, 178, 185, 187, 219
    see also LVMH

Waitrose 61
Wall Street 126–7, 143
Wal-Mart 70, 186
Warwick Business School 129
Westbrook, Daniella 206–7, 210
Westminster Council 8
Westwood, Vivienne 20, 74
Williams, Gareth 27
Williams, Matthew 159
Williamson, Matthew 159–61, 185
Wilson, Harold 129
World Intellectual Property
    Organization (WIPO) 151
World Trade Organization (WTO)
    151
Wrangler 18

Yamaha 20
Yates, Jane 26, 27
Yokohama 55–6, 190
York, Peter 182
Young, Sir George 142
Yquem 31–2
"Yuppie" 134, 137–9

Zeta-Jones, Catherine 185